The Art of Managed Services

A Practical Guide for Managed
Services Professionals

AUTHORED BY ONE OF THE MOST INSIGHTFUL
AND INFLUENTIAL PEOPLE IN THE IT CHANNEL

The Art of
Managed Services

A Practical Guide for Managed
Services Professionals

by Charles Weaver, J.D.

MSPAlliance Press

The Art of Managed Services -
A Practical Guide for Managed Services Professionals

Copyright © 2007 Charles Weaver, J.D.

Printed in the United States of America.

Published by MSPAlliance, 2595 Ceanothus Avenue Suite 180, Chico, California, 95973.

ISBN 978-1-4243-4191-7

First Edition

ABOUT THE AUTHOR

Charles Weaver is the co-founder and president of the MSP Alliance (the International Association of Managed Service Providers), with over 1400 members world wide. In addition to running the daily operational activities of the MSP Alliance, Mr. Weaver writes and speaks extensively around the world on the managed services industry. Mr. Weaver has a Bachelor of Arts degree in Political Science from Arizona State University and a Juris Doctorate from Texas Wesleyan University School of Law.

ACKNOWLEDGEMENTS

This book would never have been written if it had not been for the countless individuals I have met over the years. I must acknowledge all the thousands of conversations I have had with MSP professionals for it is really because of these conversations that I was able to form the theories that are now on these pages. While it would be impossible to mention by name all the people who made this book possible there are a few individuals I would like to mention by name because of their unique impact not only in the industry but on me personally.

I would first like to thank John Varel for his leadership and help in getting the MSPAlliance started all those years ago. I would like to acknowledge Mike Backers for his endless support of the MSPAlliance, his tireless devotion to making this industry better, and his ability to listen to me complain when I had few people to whom I could complain. Rob Scott has provided level headed advice and counsel over the years, even though our relationship began with me giving him advice. Rob, your calm and collected demeanor never ceases to amaze me; your friendship is greatly valued.

One of the numerous benefits of my becoming involved with the MSPAlliance is that I met my wife here. Celia you have been a colleague, a fellow employee, and someone who will tell me the unvarnished truth, even when it stings a little. Thank you for your support over the years. This book would never have happened without you!

This book is really dedicated to all the entrepreneurs out there who have struggled, and continue to struggle, to make this industry just a little better. There are countless MSPs and vendors who work together to create a seamless tapestry that is the managed services industry.

PREFACE

The purpose of this book is to make sense of one of the most convoluted, misinterpreted, and yet widely discussed topics in the information technology (IT) industry today: managed IT services. I began writing this book partly to memorialize some of the more common responses to questions posed to me about the managed services profession. The other reason was to clear up some of the more grotesque and damaging falsehoods that have plagued this industry for the last decade.

While this book will be of interest to many different types of readers, there are primarily two groups for whom this book was intended. The first group is comprised of those companies who are already practicing managed services providers. Most of the literature produced today is spent on helping companies get into the MSP profession. However, once this conversion has taken place very little attention is paid to those companies as they tackle the issues facing their profession. This book will attempt to provide those companies with support and guidance as existing providers of managed services.

The second group is comprised of those companies currently contemplating the transition into the managed services profession. This group of readers is certainly larger than the first group and they are arguably more vulnerable to the barrage of information being aimed at them. There is an entire industry today that sells to companies who want to become MSPs. What is most irksome to me is that many of the people now trying to sell to this group of potential MSPs are not qualified to render any advice on this complex subject matter. This group of unqualified and self proclaimed "experts" has contributed greatly to the confusion and uncertainty that exists in many young MSPs today. This book, I hope, will bring some clarity to this confusion.

The opinions expressed in this book are based on experience from close to a decade of working in the managed services profession. Many of those years have been spent talking to and analyzing how MSPs run their businesses, what their pain points are, and how the successful MSPs have achieved their success where others have not. Many of the lessons I learned came from examining how the good MSPs operated and then looking for the similarities. Many of the concepts discussed in this book are really values that many of the good MSPs have.

Another reason I decided to write this book was to correct many of the erroneous concepts that were, and still are, floating around in the managed services industry. When I say erroneous I am taking liberties because not all of the concepts contradicted in this book are erroneous. Rather, they are, in my opinion, concepts that are harmful to the managed services profession both in the near and long term. These theories tend to be offered by individuals who are just now getting into the managed services craze in order to profit from it (yes, I understand that you paid money to obtain this book). I am not against people making money. I am against people making money when it harms companies and their profession. I would hope that logic and common sense will support my theories and that my ideas will stand on their own merits.

Many of the individuals (and the theories they promote) who consult in the area of managed services tend to equate managed services with other technologies. They view managed services no differently than break/fix or reactive IT management business models. This goes a long way in explaining why they think the way they do. Most mature (and profitable) MSPs know that they are different from the reactive IT companies they used to be. They understand that the transformation process they underwent in order to become an MSP has changed them irrevocably. These MSPs tend to know that the transformation process was not something that could be pre-packaged and sold like it was some hardware appliance.

All the good MSPs (as defined by their high profit margins, high client satisfaction and retention rates, sustainable growth rates, and many other criteria) have had to work for their success. None of them bought a solution or a pre-packaged instant MSP success kit that got them to the position that they now enjoy. All of them worked hard for their success. All of them continue to work hard in order to inch closer and closer to their own ideas of managed services perfection.

The ideas discussed in this book can help you as an MSP. I know this beyond a shadow of a doubt. Naturally, just reading this book is not a guarantee of success. But by incorporating these ideas into your own managed services practice you can significantly improve your chances of achieving success in one of the most important areas impacting IT management and business today.

INTRODUCTION

Managed services are everywhere today. The term managed services, which has expanded well beyond even the information technology (IT) industry, is a global phenomenon that is as bewildering as it is lucrative. It is nearly impossible to read a technical trade magazine or web site, attend a conference, receive an email newsletter, or speak to a colleague without hearing something about managed services. And yet with all the discourse, money, and resources being spent on managed services there is still a surprisingly large amount of confusion and misinformation, especially amongst those companies considering the transition into managed services.

The IT industry, with all its hype, continues to see unprecedented growth and opportunity for those companies who have made the transition to offering managed services. And while the line of companies waiting to get into this profession continues to grow each day, the number of companies who are becoming flustered with unfulfilled promises and less than expected results also is increasing.

While managed services certainly deals with IT and how it is consumed the purpose and tone of this book is not technical in nature. Rather, the purpose of this book is to make sense of an industry that nearly everyone wants to take advantage of and yet continues to baffle individuals and companies throughout the world. To some, many of the concepts set forth in this book should seem quite commonplace, even rudimentary. To others, however, the topics will be foreign and may seem out of place in a book about the IT industry.

This book will examine several methodologies for IT services companies to enter the managed services business model. Specifically, we will look at some of the common mistakes companies make when building a managed services offering. We will also explore some of the best practices that any MSP business ought to utilize.

Although there will undoubtedly be some aspects of this book that touch on technical matters, it is not my intention to make it so. The fact that I am not a technologist should work effectively towards making the following pages very readable to both the technically proficient and laity alike. Despite the fact that many professionals employed in the IT industry will find this book of interest, there are really two groups for whom I am writing this book.

The first group is IT professionals and businesses currently providing managed services (i.e., MSPs). While some MSPs may have already encountered many of the issues addressed in this book, is very likely that the majority of MSPs in existence today have never had a clear understanding of where their industry is going or how it got there.

The second group that should read this book is the IT service providers who have not yet begun their transformation into managed services. This group, which is primarily comprised of Value Added Resellers (VARs), System Integrators (SIs), and IT consultants, has been providing valuable services to their clients for many years, but has recently seen increased pressure to deliver managed IT services. This increased pressure is very real and will likely not abate for the foreseeable future.

The issues and theories presented in this book are not complex. Yet, there is sufficient confusion in the IT industry about this topic that I felt a book like this was warranted. No matter what your views are regarding the topics discussed in this book, I would hope that the issues presented are at least discussed by businesses and organizations everywhere. While becoming an MSP is not a path for every IT services provider, it is a business model that has many benefits to it. For those that see this model as the future of IT management, then this book will hopefully serve to guide and illuminate the path ahead. For those that are just now considering this market but have not yet made up their minds, this book will either persuade or dissuade you. In that regard, no matter what decision you make, this book will have served its purpose.

MANAGED SERVICES:
A BRIEF HISTORY

In order to set the stage for the issues in this book it will be useful to look at how the IT industry has evolved over the last few decades, as well as how the consumers of IT products and services have evolved. By carefully examining these two groups and where they have come from it will become much easier to understand how their futures are tied to one another.

Technology has changed the way individuals and businesses function. Businesses can now store millions of customer files in a database or a hard drive rather than take up several store rooms of file folders. Sales teams can access corporate data from the field via secure virtual private networks (VPN). Companies can now experience and take advantage of fully integrated voice and data networks. Individuals now send electronic pictures to family members over high speed internet connections. People can now pay their bills, balance their checkbooks, buy goods and services, send email, view movies, download music, and much more, by simply taking advantage of the advancements of technology.

All these incredible technological advancements have also brought incredible confusion and uncertainty. These technologies bring great versatility and functionality as well as tremendous responsibilities. Consumers and businesses everywhere are learning about this powerful tool called IT that is now readily available to even the smallest of entities. For years now organizations have slowly become reliant on the many benefits IT can offer. Almost simultaneously, those same organizations are learning another lesson about the high cost of maintaining those IT assets. High costs of hiring talented and experienced labor, increasing government regulation and the increased liability and shame of security breaches have caused many organizations to realize the importance of maintaining effective IT management.

Before the advent of the dotcom era the threats of doing business online were minimal compared to today. Part of the reason for this is that there were far fewer networks and users back then than there are today. Today, companies and individuals who are not online are a distinct minority. This increased activity has of course caught the attention of many hackers throughout the world. The more sophisticated and mission-critical the networks and applications become the more tempted hackers are to try and break into them. In today's information age hackers operate 24-hours a day from virtually every corner of the globe. Governments, corporations, and even individuals now have to protect themselves against malicious viruses and code being hurled at them around the clock.

For many years, even before the dotcom era brought IT to the forefront of popular attention, the IT industry thrived on selling, installing, and repairing IT products for organizations. Businesses bought computers, printers, servers, and other related products from vendors who would frequently install and maintain, and upgrade those products on an ongoing basis. Leading up to and throughout the dotcom era IT maintenance became a critical item on many organizations' priority list. Organizations began to realize how important their technology was to the successful operations of their businesses.

During the last several decades it has become the norm for organizations to have dedicated in-house IT departments working for them to ensure their networks were running optimally. Issues like increased reliance on technology, e-commerce, and preparation for Y2K all had a significant impact during the 1990s on the attention paid to IT and its role in business and society.

Around this same time Application Service Providers (ASPs) started to appear offering their brand of managed services specifically related to the hosting and maintenance of business critical applications. In the next chapter we will deal with the differentiations of the numerous "xSP" acronyms that have proliferated in recent years. The genius of the ASP movement was to bring oftentimes complex and costly (to maintain) applications and deliver them to a multitude of clients via the internet. By leveraging a relationship with an ASP businesses can access these critical applications that would have previously been unavailable to them without incurring significant expense.

This same principle is what spawned the Managed Services Provider. Primarily purchased by larger enterprise clients, MSPs delivered their services also via the internet (and sometimes through the MSPs own facilities, called datacenters). Such services often included managing databases, servers, and other miscellaneous network infrastructure for clients that depended on such infrastructure yet could not manage it at the same costs as an MSP.

So why is it that these enterprise customers found managed services so appealing? There are several reasons for this. First, the tools required to manage a network back then were quite expensive. Often costing several hundred thousand in licensing fees, these powerful tools were not accessible for many companies. In addition to these powerful tools being costly to buy they were also costly to maintain. Technicians and engineers needed to install, integrate, and maintain these platforms demanded high salaries and were often rare to find.

XSP WHAT?

One of the most difficult aspects of the IT industry (or any industry for that matter) is making sense of the unique terms and phrases used in that industry. The IT industry suffers from the same confusing use of terms and phrases that often befuddle even the experts and pundits. This chapter will attempt to make some sense of what these various terms mean and how they can be distinguished from one another.

MSP (Managed Services Provider): It is appropriate that we begin with this acronym first. While there was some debate in the early years of this decade about whether MSP stood for managed or management service provider, that debate has pretty much been settled. The terms management and managed service providers are interchangeable at this juncture. The text book definition of MSP would be a company that provides predictable, proactive, managed IT services to customers on some form of recurring basis. MSPs can provide their services to their clients either remotely or at the MSP premise (usually a datacenter). More discussion regarding the terms MSP and managed services will be found later on when we examine the various forms and maturity models found in the MSP community.

ASP (Application Service Provider): ASPs were the progenitors to the MSP movement in the mid to late 1990s. ASPs host applications (usually utilizing their own servers and infrastructure) and then deliver access to that application to customers via the internet. ASPs come in many different forms and provide application services to many different markets. The Software as a Service

(SaaS) model today is really a continuation of the ASP model of yesteryear.

MSSP (Managed Security/Storage Service Provider): the acronym MSSP has been used interchangeably by both security and storage providers worldwide. While this acronym does enjoy some amount of usage, many providers simply find it expedient to use the general MSP acronym and then list the areas of their expertise separately.

VAR (Value Added Reseller): VARs resell other vendors' products and solutions, generally wrapping their own services around the sale of those solutions. VARs have existed for many years and now represent the largest body of companies transitioning to a managed services business model.[1]

System Integrators: System integrators generally work on a project basis to install and provide periodic maintenance on systems. System integrators are another large segment of companies migrating to managed services.

Utility Computing: Utility computing is a model whereby a company charges their clients for access to their IT network. Similar to how electric companies charge clients for how much energy they consume, the utility computing provider charges their clients for the actual amount of network usage they consume. In a way, the

1 It is worth noting that many thought leaders in the IT channel actually believe that VARs today are really a subset of the managed services industry. The implication here is that while VARs were the numeric majority during the 1990s, today most "VARs" are actually MSPs or making the transition into managed services.

utility computing model has quite a lot in common with the ASP model in that the client is accessing something belonging to the provider (either network access or an application) and paying for that access.

While the terms MSP and managed services have become seemingly ubiquitous of late, they are often used too liberally and some clarification is probably required at this juncture. There are many companies that provide managed services but those services represent a very small percentage of their overall revenues. Even more confusing are those companies who proclaim themselves "MSPs" when in reality they provide services that do not resemble managed services at all. Having a common nomenclature has never been a reality for this industry, and it may never be. But, by utilizing some of the definitions in this book we may be moving closer towards a common naming structure that makes sense.

At the time of writing of this book there has been a notable increase in the number of end-user consumers who are asking for MSPs and managed services by name. This will be an important trend to follow in the next several years as it will likely vindicate many of the early adopters of managed services and their decision to not only call themselves MSPs but also their decision to deliver proactive IT when many around them were not.

ORIGIN OF MANAGED SERVICES

It is difficult to understand the managed services industry of today without knowing where the industry came from and how it has progressed over the years. By understanding the origins of managed services (i.e., IT outsourcing) we can better comprehend and predict where the managed services industry is likely headed. Even more important is to know how the managed services industry has departed from the mainstream outsourcing (specifically IT outsourcing) industry and is carving a path for itself. It is this concept that is perhaps most important for the reader to understand: that managed services has, in fact, shifted dramatically away from its outsourcing roots and has now embarked upon a path that is far different from anything we have seen during the previous decades of outsourcing.

Companies have been reaping the benefits of outsourcing for decades. Starting inconspicuously with mainframe usage, companies who required large, powerful, and expensive computing power, were often forced to buy access to these computer networks on an outsourced basis. This is perhaps one of the earliest instances of a true utility computing model. In this case, the customers needed access to something that was simply beyond their financial grasp. By renting access to such a network the client had the use of the powerful computer without the massive expense of building or maintaining such an asset.

The same philosophy that applied to mainframe access was also successfully applied to other areas (some much less glamorous) such as billing, payroll, human resources, janitorial, and other non-technical services. While the cost structures may be different, the principles involved are the same. A company determines that while their need for a particular business function is great, it is not justified to bring that function in house. Instead, by outsourcing the function to an outsourcer, the company has all the benefits of the service without much of the costs and headaches of implementing and maintaining the service.

The astute reader may have realized one big difference between outsourcing use of a mainframe computer network and outsourcing a payroll service. Namely, it is much more plausible to build the internal framework for handling an organization's payroll than it was to build a mainframe network. Nevertheless, many companies decided that even with relatively simply functions like payroll and janitorial, it made more sense to hand over those duties to an outside firm rather than take on the burden of doing it themselves.

There is one very good example of business technology that has traditionally been outsourced rather than kept in-house and that is the purchase and maintenance of copiers. As early as the 1980s, organizations have been outsourcing the maintenance and procurement of copiers to third parties. Even before the computer became the cornerstone of large businesses, the copier was an essential component of many companies both large and small. Yet despite the importance of copiers to many companies very few of them actually purchased and maintained that equipment themselves. Today, copiers share many similarities with computers. Copiers can connect to a network and communicate with other devices, not to mention share many of the same vulnerabilities that plague IT networks.

While there is no precise date we can pinpoint as the first time managed services as a term or a business model was employed we can narrow it down to sometime in the early to mid-1990s. What is more likely the case is that the business model came into existence far before the term managed services began to enjoy widespread usage. One would have to do a fair amount of investigative research in order defined as a term MSP or managed services in the technical trade journals and magazines of the last decade. What is certain is that around the turn of the millennium the managed services industry was experiencing noticeable coverage by the technical press as well as adoption by some of the early MSP pioneers.

MANAGED SERVICES DURING THE 1990S

Thus far we have examined the origins of outsourcing throughout the decades and how it became an acceptable, if not a necessary practice for many organizations. During the 1990s, when IT began to gain widespread adoption and usage, the large enterprise took the same approach to IT as it did with copiers, HR, and other traditionally outsourced functions. It is during this time that large organizations began to truly rely on IT in a way that they had never done in the past. Or perhaps it is just that there were more companies using IT than there had been before. Personal computers, more powerful processors, geographically diverse networks, and other technological advancements promised a new way to conduct business.

This new way of conducting business, while exciting and full of promise, brought with it a new set of headaches and challenges for the companies implementing such a strategy. Access to human resources was typically at the top of the list of challenges. Assuming that the organization had the financial resources it was not always possible to hire all the talent needed to effectively manage the large and often complex IT infrastructure.

Access to tools was another hindrance to effective IT management. Even if the company had the necessary staff, having access to the proper tools was another question altogether. During this period there were very few software and hardware tools available to manage complex IT networks and the ones that were available were often very expensive. High licensing costs coupled with complex and lengthy integration procedures created difficulties even for the largest and most financially well-off institutions.

It is during the same time that the first MSPs began to sprout up. Very similar to their mainframe outsourcing cousins, the MSPs of the 90s have access to all the necessary tools and human resources required to those tools to use. And so these MSPs began to "rent" their tools and human resources to large enterprises that had the need for such resources but did not want to expend the financial capital in order to access them.

As many of you reading this book may well remember, around this same time the application service provider also came into existence. Companies soon found that the same logic that they had applied towards copiers and general IT infrastructure could also be applied towards applications. Large enterprises often needed specific applications for their businesses. These applications were by no means cheap. Either they were costly to license (in the case of off-the-shelf applications) or they had to be custom programmed. In the case of custom-designed applications, because there was no company behind that application to support it on an ongoing basis, the company typically had to hire the original developers (if they provided such support) or other IT providers to maintain and improve these applications.

While this practice certainly continues today, in the case of commonly used applications such as CRM, ERP, e-commerce, and similar programs that were used widely by many different companies, ASPs began the unique service of hosting an application (using their own IT infrastructure) and making it available to many different clients on a recurring revenue basis. Therefore, instead of a company having to go out and buy or develop a customer relationship management software platform, they could subscribe to a service which gave them all the functionality of that application without having to build or maintain the infrastructure required to host it, not to mention the resources and cost involved in creating or buying that application in the first place.

Once again, the practice of engaging a third-party in order to leverage their expertise and access resources was met with very little resistance. The primary reason for this near universal acceptance was that the consumers (in this case large enterprises) were entities that absolutely needed this technology in order to function and were unwilling to spend the money to build and maintain the necessary infrastructure. During this time, the small to medium sized business market was generally unaware of this practice, or if they were aware, they were not utilizing IT in the same way as their enterprise counterparts.

Now for many of you who may be wondering which came first, the MSP or ASP, we will address this question at this point. In all honesty, it is likely irrelevant which business model came first. While there are some instances of managed service providers as far back as the early 1990s, the term MSP was not widely used. In fact, it is very likely that the term ASP found widespread adoption and usage several years before the term MSP. Regardless of which term came into popular usage first, it is widely acknowledged that the managed services business model actually came into existence first. It is simply one of those ironic twists of fate that the ASP acronym began to get press coverage prior to the MSP acronym.

THE PROSPERITY OF THE 1990S

It is impossible to examine the 1990s without addressing the frenzy that surrounded the technology sector at that time. In a decade that saw an incredible level of economic growth and prosperity (at least for a good part of the decade) there was also an incredible amount of buzz and activity in the technology sector, specifically technologies that involved the Internet.

One possible explanation for the hype that existed during the mid-to late 1990s, particularly in Silicon Valley, is the unusually high flow of investment capital that was spent in the technology sector. Venture Capital firms were abundant and they were more than willing to fund any business that even smacked of the Internet. Entrepreneurs (particularly those engaged in technology and the Internet), including some with very little business experience, could write a business idea on a napkin and it would get funding. While it is not the purpose of this book to examine the shortcomings of the venture capital industry during the mid to late 1990s, it is important to have some perspective in order to understand the environment in which some of the first mainstream MSPs got their start.[2]

In the middle of the booming ASP market we saw the emergence of the first MSPs with true international notoriety. These companies, primarily built around large data centers designed to host and manage infrastructure, received a great deal of attention from the venture capitalists and analysts. The reason for this is very simple: the early MSPs required large financial investments in order to function. MSP facilities were often

---

2 The venture capital fiasco combined with the failure of the dotcom years of the 1990s has yielded a much more practical and realistic investment community in the new millennium.

very large and replete with extraordinary security and redundancy features. As discussed previously, the remote monitoring and management platforms that were available during this time were very costly to license, maintain, and integrate.

As was quite typical during this time, these early MSPs were obliged to spend large sums of money before they even had their first clients. When they did acquire new clients they usually came at a cost. The enterprise clients these early MSPs sought, while ideal candidates for managed services, usually had lengthy sales cycles. Keep in mind that this era of managed services was not without its problems. Directors of IT, who were very often the target of managed services sales personnel, were very often threatened by the notion of managed services. To them, the concept of outsourcing even a portion of their IT infrastructure was a threat to their existence. More than anything, it was a general lack of understanding on the part of enterprise consumers that hindered many managed services relationships during these years.

At the time of this writing there are very few of these early MSPs still in existence. Many were lost to bankruptcies and acquisitions, while the few that did remain had to radically cut back and adapt in order to survive the lean years that lay ahead of them. Later in this book we will examine more closely some of the failings of these early MSPs but suffice it to say that this era of MSP did lay the foundation for the managed services industry of the new millennium.

Y2K AND THE ECONOMIC RECESSION

For several years leading up to the new millennium people were confused and concerned about what this important milestone would bring. Vast sums of money were spent on IT companies and consultants in an attempt to prepare for the "Y2K bug". In the end, nothing of significance really happened except maybe some shattered opinions how useful IT really was. And whether it was Y2K, a stock market with exaggerated valuations, a lack of trust in the new economy and political administration, or a combination of all these factors, consumer IT spending quickly slowed and the first wave of MSPs soon found themselves fighting for their lives.

There is little dispute that the economic downturn was already well underway before the September 11 attacks happened. If there was any hope of a quick economic recovery it was certainly shattered that day. It would be improper to place too much importance on the September 11 attacks as the sole reason for the economic troubles that soon followed. To say that it was a reason (perhaps even a big reason) goes without saying, but whatever the factors involved it is a fact that the global economy suffered in the years immediately following the new millennium until at least the second or third quarter of 2003.

During this stretch of time the early MSPs went through severe contractions as they struggled to stay alive when very few end-user organizations were spending any money. Many of these early MSPs went on life support fueled by the cash reserves they had received from their venture capital investments. But even these large sums of money would eventually run out someday. As these difficult months dragged on we saw many MSP is begin to go out of business or become acquired by other MSPs who were simply looking for any way to prop up their businesses long enough to survive the economic drought.

Merger and acquisition activity during this period was often frenetic and without any rhyme or reason. Valuations of businesses plummeted or were immediately discounted when revenue was not tied to an agreement.

It is also worth pointing out that the managed services industry never went away during the economic recession. Rather, it experienced a period of significant hardship both from within as well as outside. As will be discussed in greater detail in the next chapter, MSPs that were either created during this time or were still holding on from the dotcom era faced many challenges.

THE NEW ERA OF MANAGED SERVICES

The post September, 11 2001 MSP was a much leaner, more adaptive, agile, and profitable species than their 20th century era cousins. The MSPs today are much more vibrant and multifaceted in the sheer breadth of offerings and market verticals they service. The combination of increased regulation and massive global adoption of IT has caused the largest growth of managed services consumption and a corresponding increase in the number of companies that are transitioning into or starting up managed services firms.

MSPs today are spreading into the remotest regions of the world, even those regions that do not yet have fully mature infrastructures. The enterprise and mid-market consumers, while no strangers to managed services, continue to experience very respectable adoption. Yet it is the small to medium sized business community (SMB) that has proven to be the most lucrative and sensational market in the last 5 years.

The SMB market was never considered a viable consumer of managed services before the new millennium. And although the mid-market and enterprise sectors still consume managed services, the most money being spent on managed services and technology as a whole is and will likely remain the SMB market. Therefore, we will spend a little time examining the reasons for this explosive growth, looking into why SMB focused MSPs are having difficulties making the transition into managed services, as well as the future that lies ahead for the MSP community.

MANAGED SERVICES GOES SMB

It is likely that very few SMB focused IT solution providers, VARs, and system integrators have not heard about managed services. Much of the dialog today surrounding managed services is focused on why companies should start a managed services practice. Why such a stark change from just a few years earlier when only the large and well funded could enter this profession? Service enabling technology vendors have revolutionized this industry in a way that may never be appreciated or understood.

The MSPs of the 1990s had very powerful, expensive, and complex tools at their disposal. More importantly, there were not that many network and systems management tools in existence during that period. As a result, there were probably fewer than a hundred true MSPs around during the late 1990s.

After the new millennium, a handful of small yet inventive companies began manufacturing powerful, lightweight, easier to use, and inexpensive tools specifically for smaller MSPs. These service enabling vendors were pioneers in creating tools for the SMB market when the SMB managed services market did not even exist at the time. Advancements included basic network and system management, desktop management, to very robust security solutions that were created in response to the growing threat of IT security. Remote connectivity, disparate office branches, mobile workforce, and increased demand for high performance applications are just a few of the many service enabling technologies that were suddenly available to smaller MSPs (primarily those focused on servicing the SMB market).

Regardless of whether these companies were responsible for the growth we see today or because they were simply responding to nascent demand we may never know. It is not in dispute, however, that without these advancements in service enabling technologies the MSP industry of today would not be where it is.

IT COMES UNDER ATTACK

The widespread growth of managed services is not just a product of technological advancement. The first few years of this decade saw a remarkable adoption of IT by the consumer market (both domestic and corporate users). Slowly but surely, words like spyware, computer viruses, spam, hacking, data breach, and denial of service began to creep into the popular lexicon. Daily news programs would regularly feature some story about a company being hacked, or a new virus that hit the Internet causing massive damage and mayhem. Technology and its vulnerabilities, perhaps for the first time ever, became something that everyday people were used to seeing and hearing.

With the widespread popularity and comfort with technology also came the problems. Uneducated consumers, both at home and at the office, began to use IT without fully appreciating the complexities involved in maintaining IT. Neither did these consumers fully understand the risks of an unprotected network. Domestic users and small offices became the targets for both those that would try and destroy the network as well as to those vendors that manufactured tools to help protect those networks. Intrusion detection, anti-virus, anti-spyware, backup and storage, and many other products and solutions began to appear everywhere.

The de facto standard during these early days of massive IT adoption and usage was what is popularly referred to as break/fix or reactive IT management. Simply stated break/fix IT management is responding to a consumer complaint about their IT after the problem has already happened. For example, if a small office experienced an outage of their email, they would typically call a break/fix IT shop to come in and repair it. In these situations, the IT provider would physically send a technician out to the customer premise and fix the problem. The most popular style of billing for this style of IT management would be hourly. In some cases there are early examples of IT providers selling their clients blocks of time which simply meant that the consumer could receive some form of discount in exchange for buying a larger block of time than they would normally purchase. Regardless of the billing method the consumer was still reacting to IT problems. They may have felt better about their IT assets but in the end, the network most likely had to fail before the break/fix company would be able to remediate it.

During the last seven years it is undeniable that the SMB end-user consumer market began to experience significant pain around their IT assets as they came under increased attack from a variety of intentional and unintentional sources.

IT IS REGULATED

Several years into the new millennium the real impact of unmanaged IT began to emerge as a problem that would garner significant public debate. While IT regulation has been around for many years, the significance of IT in the public eye was definitely increasing in the new millennium. Laws such as the Health Insurance Portability and Accountability Act of 1996 (HIPAA), Gramm Leach Bliley Act (GLBA), Sarbanes-Oxley, SEC regulation 17a-4, and many others began to have real and often costly consequences for corporations everywhere.

Once again, the widespread increase in IT usage was the major reason for the severity of the impact these laws were having on corporations. For example, as the healthcare community continues to strive each day towards greater adoption of electronic medical records, healthcare professionals are struggling with how to incorporate technology without having it become a burden. Similarly, in other industries like the legal profession, IT has brought significant advancements to the practice of law. Areas such as online research, communication, and litigation applications have all made the practice of law easier in many ways. Yet, with all these advancements, the issue of data privacy and its implications on the attorney client privilege remain of great concern to many practicing attorneys.

Perhaps this is no great revelation that advancements in technology also bring headaches and problems. However, what is perhaps unique to the IT industry is that the advancements in IT and its increased adoption by everyday consumers has brought a lot of scrutiny on how IT is being used and how data is being protected. As legislators across the world begin to fully comprehend how wide spread and potentially dangerous unmanaged IT can be, more laws will be enacted to combat data loss.

The trend of IT regulation will only continue as IT becomes more entrenched in society. The overall issue of how data is being stored, who is seeing it, and how it is being stored, will likely be the preeminent subject of debate as lawmakers the world over come to grips with IT management.

MANAGED SERVICES VS. IT OUTSOURCING

In the previous chapter we briefly discussed several of the more common acronyms and terms used in the IT industry. In this chapter, I would like to cover the broader issue of IT outsourcing. This term is a macro concept that has consumed many pages of commentary, countless hours of discourse, and plenty of money spent (both by industry insiders as well as IT consumers) in order to make sense of this widely used yet misunderstood concept.

During the nascent years of the managed services industry the term IT outsourcing and managed services were often used interchangeably. While the two terms may have at one time shared similarities the managed services industry has made (and is making) significant strides to divorce itself from the generic IT outsourcing industry. The early years of this millennium saw a great amount of press attention (both in the technical as well as mainstream press) on the subject of outsourcing. For a few years the issue of off shoring to countries such as India was a political hot potato that very few politicians wanted to touch.

What confused many people during this period was the interchangeable use of the term off shoring with outsourcing. Invariably, when this topic was written about or discussed by the news media date were referencing the political effect of off shoring and how this practice was impacting US jobs. While this may have, and perhaps still is, a legitimate point of issue and debate there is very little evidence to suggest that managed services ever had a negative impact on the job market either domestically or abroad. Only when discussing very large outsourcing projects that specifically deal with replacing thousands of employees with outsourced labor does the issue of job security and stability become an issue.[3]

Nevertheless, the mainstream and technical press during these years did an effective job of confusing the issue of outsourcing, IT outsourcing, offshoring, and managed IT services. Many MSPs during this time reported having difficulty in educating their clients about the nature of their services when many of these clients were reading press articles talking about the dangers of doing business with outsourcing firms. In hindsight it is very easy to understand why this confusion existed. In today's global economy we do see emerging trends in the acceptance of off shoring and international partnerships between MSPs, especially when they involve larger projects. However, it should be made perfectly clear that off shoring and outsourcing in general have very little to do with the profession of delivering managed IT services.

---

3 Offshoring has traditionally not implicated the managed services profession. Instead, it has more to do with regular outsourcing than anything else.

THE POLITICS OF IT OUTSOURCING

IT outsourcing has long been a resource accessed by businesses everywhere. Common services consumed by IT outsourcing clients, starting with the early days of mainframe rental, included software development, remote monitoring, staffing, and other high demand IT services. The IT outsourcing industry of 5 years ago began to experience rapid growth abroad, particularly from countries outside North America. To make the issue even more confusing, the term offshoring began to be used interchangeably with IT outsourcing. The reason for this confusion was really due to the increasing political pressure offshoring experienced several years ago.

As politicians began to contemplate how offshoring was affecting US jobs, the tech media began to write more on the increasingly controversial subject. As more articles and commentary began to surface the offshoring name started to become intertwined with IT outsourcing. Soon pundits, writers, analysts, and other self proclaimed industry experts began to inject IT outsourcing with all the negative attributes of the offshoring industry. This is just one reason why the managed services industry began to move away from IT outsourcing.

While it is not the intention of this book to in any way critique the offshoring industry, it is important to understand how much of the tech media (including some analysts and industry pundits) began to confuse end-user consumers by attributing pejorative characteristics of offshoring to the IT outsourcing industry as a whole. This practice, while not practiced much today, was a leading reason for many in the managed services industry to start thinking of themselves as different from generic IT outsourcing providers. Perhaps as a marketing effort, but more likely as a philosophical departure from what many in the IT outsourcing industry were preaching, the managed services leadership began to see fundamental differences in how others viewed their industry.

The majority of offshoring proponents were in favor of the model primarily for economic reasons. Offshoring reached the zenith of its popularity during some of the bleakest economic times here in the United States. The dotcom fallout, September 11, 2001, the economic slowdown, and other factors provided the offshoring model with merit. During this time period many offshoring IT providers, primarily from India but also from other parts of the Asia Pacific region began to show interest in selling their services to the West. At the time, the difference between Asia Pacific region IT salaries and Western IT salaries was significant. As a result, many corporations found the cost saving benefits to offshoring certain elements of their IT and business processes very compelling. In particular, application development projects began to steadily drift to overseas firms who promised high value programmers at very affordable prices.

This focus on price as a determining factor of choosing an IT provider struck a very negative chord in many North American MSPs. In part, this was a reaction to a slow economy and difficult sales cycles. The separation from offshoring was also a factor of many MSPs not wanting to see their services evaluated on price.[4] For a while, many MSPs actually began calling themselves IT outsourcing providers. But as the line of offshoring companies grew and their presence in the US became more pronounced, soon many MSPs saw an advantage to distinguishing themselves from the IT outsourcing providers. While price can be an influential sales and marketing tool for some MSPs today, there are numerous benefits to managed services that have very little to do with actual cost savings for the consumer.

The relationship between offshoring and managed services will likely continue for the foreseeable future but with the notable changes. First, most offshoring relationships today are based on geographic and time factors. For example, an MSP in North America can have clients all over the world by leveraging multiple Network Operation Centers both domestically and overseas. Such a setup can afford the MSP true 24/7 monitoring and management capabilities as well as bring some measure of cost savings through cheaper overseas labor.[5] Second, due to increasing global security concerns many governments are limiting the types of IT related outsourcing to foreign entities. As the trend towards greater transparency between clients and their MSPs continue, the practice of inserting multiple firms into a managed services relationship will be carried out with great discretion. While there is plenty of important IT functions that will continue to be leveraged via offshore relationships the trend will likely be that more sensitive IT managed services will remain within the client/MSP country.

4 This is perhaps one of the first signs of the MSPs rejecting the notion of managed services as a commodity.
5 While impossible to predict future global economic conditions at the time of this writing the differences between North American and Asia Pacific wages have narrowed considerably and show continuing signs of equalization. As a result of this trend the marketing strategies of many offshore IT providers has changed, relying less on financial cost savings and more on technical proficiency, education, and 24/7 operational functionality.

MANAGED SERVICE PROVIDERS GROW UP

One of the first signs that the managed services industry was maturing was the act of separating itself from the IT outsourcing industry at large. While there are plenty of reasons why this happened the important point to understand is that IT outsourcing and managed services have both taken different paths despite a common origination point. It would not be accurate to say that MSPs became who they were just because they wanted a marketing scheme to distinguish themselves from other IT outsourcing providers. Instead, at the same time the offshoring model was taking its worst hits politically, the MSP model was just beginning to take hold in the SMB market. Thousands of IT solution providers were beginning to hear about the benefits of making the transition into managed services. This new profession for SMB IT providers was very powerful and prompted many of them to change their business models, invest in new tools, and develop new methodologies for delivering services to their clients.

Another reason for the departure from IT outsourcing was the increasing complexity of IT management issues. As regulation, IT security, and corporate governance became more stringent, the concept of handing over vital parts of a company's IT management to an IT outsourcing provider seemed misguided, especially when those same IT providers were selling their services as a cost benefit. Companies started seeing their IT management needs in a different light. No longer were they simply looking for a technological fix; what they wanted was a business solution. The IT outsourcing providers that primarily focused on price differentiators couched their solutions as technical in nature with very little emphasis or discussion on how it would affect the client's business. MSPs began to look at IT not as a technical problem but as a business problem. This change in thinking marked one of the seminal shifts in how MSPs and IT outsourcing providers viewed technology.

As will be discussed in the next chapter, the increasing pressure of legislative regulation on IT departments forced many MSPs to expand their expertise to non-technical areas that affected IT. Security audits, forensic security services, complex backup and archiving solutions, and many other services began to be offered with special attention paid to the impact of IT on the business objectives of the company. This shift in offering more business type services only furthered the separation between the MSPs and other reactive IT providers.

Another interesting facet of the managed services profession that has developed over the years is the level of intimacy and trust most clients have with their MSPs. Going well past the traditional relationship between IT solution provider and their clients many MSPs will tell you that their clients place a great deal of reliance on the MSPs advice and counsel. So great is this level of trust that the MSPs naturally are drawn into more situations thereby having a greater impact on the client's IT and business goals. This trend has caused the MSPs to have to become well versed on subject matter areas that have traditionally not had much place in the mainstream IT solution provider world.

Maturation of the managed services industry has been and continues to be one of the primary objectives within the managed services industry. Of particular challenge is the increasing number of new MSPs entering the industry. These young and inexperienced MSPs need higher levels of education and peer mentoring in order to achieve even a minimal level of managed services competency. While the high adoption rates of the managed services profession is a very encouraging sign the industry must find ways to educate these new MSPs, not only for the sake of their clients but also for the sake of the entire industry.

Today, more money and resources are being spent on managed services education than has ever been spent before. Primarily fueled by vendors wishing to capitalize on the managed services craze, the number of educational tools and resources is staggering. And while the amount of education is very encouraging the pace still needs to be faster. At the current rate end-user consumers are in danger of growing at a faster rate than the qualified MSPs. Because end-users are beginning to demand managed services from their IT providers there has never been a more important time for managed services education. As the demand for managed services continues to rise so will the frenzy (on the part of the IT solution providers) to enter the managed services profession.

MANAGED SERVICES AND THE LAW

Today, the law and IT are increasingly becoming intertwined in very complex ways. This chapter will examine how legislatures around the world are taking action in order to protect the data integrity of their citizenry, not to mention other areas that impact IT security and public safety. While this section may seem beyond the scope of what an MSP should know the issues discussed here are quite important to managed services professionals everywhere. It is probably safe to say that these legal issues discussed in this chapter are becoming mandatory learning for today's MSP.

Because of the unique intersection of law and IT, there is an emerging trend where IT professionals are learning more about the law and legal professionals are learning more about IT management. While the outcome of this trend is uncertain, for the foreseeable future both legal and IT professionals will become heavily reliant on one another as both industries come to grips with the ever evolving complexities of IT management and the legal ramifications that surround it .

REGULATION AND MANAGED SERVICES

The managed services revolution would not be what it is today if it had not been for the dramatic increase in governmental regulation on IT usage and management. Since the mid to late 1990s, governmental bodies (including, but not limited to the United States government) have been slowly but surely coming to grips with the threat of unmanaged IT. The steady increase in the amount of regulations affecting, either directly or indirectly, IT is showing no signs of slowing. These legislative attempts to curb abuses and harm to the public general appear after well publicized events that impact either IT security or data privacy. While these laws are well intending they have been rather short sighted in cases where the legislative body reacts very quickly to a perceived threat but without all the information necessary to draft an intelligent and forward thinking piece of legislation. Because of the rapid pace of IT advancement worldwide, legislative bodies will always face the challenge of creating laws that not only protect the general public, but do so without unnecessarily harming the very industry that seeks to achieve the very same objective. California Senate Bill 1386 (which later became law) was one such example of a legislature taking action before all the facts had been collected.

California SB 1386 was an attempt to proscribe (or at least curb) the spyware and adware programs there were proliferating all over the world during the first few years of this century. Spyware and adware at the time, and continue even today, was a plague for business and consumer users everywhere by exposing sensitive consumer data, compromising IT networks, and in general letting everyone know that technology had risks that were not exclusive to the large corporate infrastructures.

The public response (to the extent that they understood what it was about) to the California legislature's efforts was by and large positive. Viewed as a tangible response by the law makers to protect California citizenry from malicious programs CA. SB 1386 was a step in the right direction according to the general public. However, the IT community thought differently. The way the bill was written would have proscribed many legitimate programs commonly used by MSPs to provide their services to their clients. Specifically, these programs (that would have been labeled spyware under this proposed legislation) are necessary tools used by MSPs to actually identify and catch spyware, adware, and other malicious programs. Through the efforts of several large corporations and IT industry bodies (including the MSPAlliance) the bill was amended to exempt such organizations from the reach of the bill. Eventually the bill passed the state congress and was signed into law by Governor Arnold Schwarzenegger.

SB 1386 was the first of its kind in the United States. It was an important piece of legislation for consumers and a good model for other states (and the federal government) to copy for their own versions of anti-spyware bills. It was, however, a near miss in the eyes of many IT professionals. The bill was a glaring example of how much the IT community needs to be aware of and involved in the legislative process when it comes to IT management. The fact that technology is always one step ahead of the general public demands that the IT community properly inform the public sector of what is going on at all times. The presence of IT in our daily lives is undisputed. However, there is still a large gap in the education of everyday users about how important and potentially dangerous unmanaged IT can be. Education must rule the day if the threat of unmanaged IT has any hope of being conquered.

Over the years similar pieces of legislation (while not directly aimed at IT) have had a significant impact on IT usage and management. The Health Insurance Privacy and Portability Act of 1996 (HIPPA) continues to have a significant impact on the healthcare industry. Primarily concerned with patient privacy HIPPA has been a consuming point of discussion for the medical establishment. Large hospitals all the way down to small private practices have heard of HIPPA and know its importance. What is generally not known is the practical: how to secure patient records and make IT work for the medical community instead of being a hindrance. The push to make medical records electronic only compounds the problem. Over the next few years the medical and IT communities will be working very closely to create a solution to this problem.[6]

Similarly, laws such as Gramm-Leach-Bliley, Securities and Exchange Commission Regulation 17a-4, Sarbanes-Oxley, and others, have applied tremendous pressure on the financial services industry to ensure that IT is being used properly. Late in 2006, the Federal Rules of Civil Procedure were amended

6 Several countries, including the UK, have already begun the process of moving towards electronic medical records.

to include new rules related to e-discovery. In specific, these new rules impact how evidence is collected and produced during civil litigation. In the past, when litigants to a civil action prepared for trial, they used the process of discovery to obtain important information and evidence that may be used during the trial. Failure to produce documents (or even worse, the act of destroying evidence during this process) resulted in stiff penalties. The latest e-discovery rules now apply to electronic information and evidence.

For example, if a company was going to trial and was compelled to disclose certain information in its possession that company would comb through their files and produce (in some cases) large volumes of paperwork. As more and more companies are relying less on paper and more on electronic records, they now have to treat such electronic records just as they did the paper records. Only no longer will companies have the excuse that their IT department did not know how to properly archive their email. Failure to produce these electronic files will be just as severe as if the company failed to produce the paper records. Such a rule impacts all companies, large and small as well as public and private. And while the onslaught of legislation is certainly the highest in the US, it would be improper to say that IT legislation is not occurring globally. Many countries, including the European Union, are producing their own versions of legislative protection for IT security and data privacy.

It is worth noting at this point that the underlying theme in most of the IT legislation today deals with the issue of data privacy. While spyware, adware, SPAM, denial of service attacks, and many other technologies are being addressed, they all represent attacks on the data privacy of individuals and organizations everywhere. We continue to see a rise in the amount of phishing, electronic extortion, and intellectual property theft as well. These crimes, while having deep roots, are increasingly utilizing the Internet and other electronic methods for reaching their victims. This is a trend that will likely continue for the foreseeable future. Data privacy is at the heart of all IT; if the privacy of someone's data cannot be secured then IT is not working. Data privacy and protection is the central challenge of IT management as well as the credo of the managed services industry.

THE LIABILITY OF IT

Perhaps no area of jurisprudence has been as misunderstood as information technology. A big reason for this lack of understanding is the rapid pace at which technology advances. By the time a legal issue has had the chance to work its way through the legal system technology has changed the subject. This is the nature of technology and it will likely not ever change.

While IT regulation has been written about and discussed ad nauseum in recent years the issue of legal liability for mismanagement of IT has been largely overlooked. It is possible that the lack of understanding of how technology works, combined with a lack of meaningful legal discussion, has made the legal community reluctant to embrace technology (both as users as well as litigators). One possible reason for the lack of any significant IT case law could be due to the absence of any IT management standard.

IT management standards tend to be prevalent primarily among the IT professionals. Naturally, many of us would not think this odd. However, the previous inability of IT professionals to bridge the gap between IT and business has been a problem. This gap, as should be quite evident having read this book up to this point, is being bridged by the MSP community. In fact, it has been the MSP profession that has had the most impact on helping the business community bridge IT management standards into effective business solutions. Later on in the book we will examine several of the more prominent IT management standards and the level of success each has had in becoming adopted by the mainstream business community. For the time being, let us resolve that the legal community has had very little assistance from the IT community when it comes to IT management standards that can be used to create any meaningful legal precedent.

Because technology has been so misunderstood for so many years, it is difficult for most people, including businesses, to come to grips with how powerful IT really is. More importantly, many people do not realize the damage that can occur when IT is left unmanaged or is mismanaged. The majority of people today view computers as sometimes useful machines that frequently break. Even the smallest of companies today often have complex and powerful IT networks that frequently do not support the business objectives in the way that they should. But the issue of an unguarded IT network as a potential for legal liability has probably not entered the minds of many small business owners and CEOs.

While most of us understand that leaving a loaded firearm out in plain sight is not a good thing to do there have been plenty of examples where such behavior has resulted in prosecution and/or civil action when harm has resulted from a firearm that was improperly secured. The result should be no different with IT. Although we have not seen a flurry of civil litigation or criminal prosecution of corporate executives who have mismanaged IT networks it will only take a few examples before every corporate executive begins to take precautions.[7]

Most of the pressure businesses receive today comes from areas of specific federal or state regulation (i.e., HIPPA, GLBA, SEC Reg. 17a-4, etc). What many businesses do not perceive today is the potential for huge legal liability for failing to adequately manage and protect their IT networks. It is only a matter of time before widespread civil litigation (and potentially criminal action) comes to businesses of all sizes for failure to adequately protect their IT assets.

Corporate malfeasance is another area where many corporate executives are woefully ignorant. Because many executives do not have very good insight into their IT infrastructure they

---

7 There have already been notable examples of large corporate penalties incurred for failure to produce electronic records due to substandard data storage and archiving policies.

are unaware of the many problems that may be going on within their own organization.

For example, most employees understand that stealing paperclips, staplers, or other property belonging to the company for which they work would be an offence punishable by fines, demotion, or even termination. Executives tend to pay close attention to theft of corporate property. But when it comes to malfeasance involving corporate IT a blind eye is often turned; in many cases, the blind eye is a result of ignorance on the part of the executives.

Employees who conduct personal business over the internet, download non-work related items, play games, or perform many other tasks that not only chew up corporate resources but also squander their own time when they should be working are just as guilty as those employees who are caught with their hand in the corporate cookie jar. But because many executives, particularly those who run small and medium sized businesses, do not have the tools, man power, or knowledge to identify such behavior a solution will rarely be found. After all, is an employee who downloads massive files (for personal use) at work causing the entire company network to screech to a halt any different than an employee who was pilfering company office supplies?

While most executives would be upset to know that their employees are squandering company resources and time these same executives would likely be furious to know that their employees were committing illegal acts using corporate resources. There have been numerous examples of sexual harassment, child pornography, and other prurient or criminal acts being committed by employees at work. In many of the cases, it is an MSP who finds evidence of such wrongdoing and brings it to the attention of the executive branch. Just as employers can be held liable for failure to take action when employees bring examples of wrongdoing to their attention, so will these executives be liable when the wrongdoing is committed using a computer.

The likely future for litigation involving IT is negligence. While this is an area well known to civil litigators, IT negligence has had relatively little interactivity with corporations. Lack of a strong IT management standard, difficulty with collecting IT evidence, and overall IT inexperience has caused many in the legal industry to view IT as a dark and unknown frontier. Corporate executives view IT negligence in much the same way. The inability of most organizations to make IT work towards their business objectives precludes their executives from knowing when their IT is exposing them to potential legal troubles. In this one area, MSPs have the potential to do the most good for their clients.

Leaders within the MSP industry are even now contemplating the ever expanding role of MSPs and how they should be serving their clients. One such area involves the issue of client/MSP confidentiality. Other professions (like legal, medical, and psychiatry) rely on privileged information in order to perform their obligations to their clients. The ability to hear and keep certain information private is a critical component for many professionals as they assist their clients. There are many reasons for creating privilege between professional and client but all of them tend to support the effectiveness of the professional in their rendering of advice and counsel to their clients. The same is true with managed services relationships. Particularly in a time when many executives are going to begin realizing how exposed they really are, they will need to rely on the privileged relationship with their MSP in order to achieve a resolution to their problems.

One example of how privilege can be useful to MSPs involves discovery of compromising situations within the client's organization. During the course of a routine IT audit an MSP can uncover a wealth of information about the client. MSPs frequently discover discrepancies in software licensing, gaps in the client's IT security, even identify employees who misuse corporate IT assets. Organizations who have unlicensed copies of software may want to rectify the situation by purchasing the appropriate licenses. Companies may find out that their IT perimeter has been penetrated and that sensitive data has been compromised. Still other organizations may find out that their employees are engaged in misconduct that could harm the organization by making them liable. Companies will be less likely to be open if they feel that their MSP will compromise or harm them by disclosing sensitive information to third parties.

The ability of MSPs to see cracks in the IT armor of their clients will be very important in future years as corporations everywhere learn about the perils of unmanaged IT. The future will undoubtedly bring more responsibility and liability to organizations with regards to their IT. Specifically in the area of data privacy corporations will no longer be able to have the excuse of "I didn't know what was happening." Even the smallest companies will have no place to hide from the law when IT management and data privacy become front page news. Consumers who are the victims of data loss will demand action from any organization that does not take minimal steps to safeguard their privacy. This includes both civil litigation as well as potential criminal action. The more the general public is aware of the perils of mismanaged IT the more MSPs will become critical to businesses everywhere.

In a later chapter we will discuss the professional and ethical obligations MSPs have when they uncover corporate wrongdoing, including appropriate steps they should take.

BECOMING AN MSP

Perhaps no topic of conversation has more occupied the IT channel for the last several years than how to become a managed service provider. And yet, while this topic has been at the forefront of the IT channel it is doubtful that there are many other issues more misunderstood than managed services. While the first part of this book has been spent defining terms, providing historical context, and clarifying concepts, the second part will focus primarily on practical recommendations for building a successful managed services practice.

As has been previously discussed, there are many different varieties of MSP in existence today. Many differences can be attributed to service and market verticals while others are far more subtle, like geographic and cultural variations. Despite these many subtle differences this section will attempt to outline some of the more mainstream challenges and solutions faced by companies today who are trying to build a managed services practice. It is impossible to account for each and every business that is out there but the following concepts should be applicable to most companies evaluating or currently undergoing the managed services transformation process.

It is important to note that many of the theories in this section, while having been proven over the years, may require subtle manipulation in order to make them work for your particular company. During the years I have seen many variations of MSP and a similar number of variations when it came to how they achieved their success. While some MSPs were able to successfully build their own technology platforms, others needed to purchase one "off the shelf". Some MSPs successfully transitioned their existing clients over a very short period of time while others took considerably longer. I am convinced that management styles mean everything when building a managed services practice. Each of us is different in how we organize, think, and operate. In short, how we relate to others is as unique as our DNA. I have seen MSPs break the mold when building their managed services practice, seemingly leaving conventional wisdom behind them.

In the end, results are what matter the most here. The ability to build (either from the ground up or by transforming your current IT services business) a managed services firm often stems from the ability of the executives to structure a plan and effectively see that plan through to fruition. The philosophies embedded in this book have been extracted from real life examples and distilled to the point where they should be applicable to many different scenarios. However, it is entirely plausible that you may read these theories, take what you need from them and then create your own path towards a managed services firm. This is perfectly acceptable.

The managed services industry has traveled great distances since its inception and much of the reason for this progress has been the ingenuity and resourcefulness of the executives. Their need to achieve results has, in many cases, caused them to think outside the box and create solutions to problems where previously there had been no solution.

Whatever path you end up choosing there is one principle that is not in dispute and that is the professionalism, integrity, and ethical behavior that are demanded of you as a member of the managed services industry. On these traits there can be no circumvention.

BREAKING FREE OF THE REACTIVE CULTURE

The managed services profession is about giving organizations IT that supports and furthers their business objectives. While the notion of functioning IT may not be a novel one it is certainly a concept that has been elusive of most companies today. What has become patently clear to many in the IT industry is that reactive IT management is no longer acceptable. This simple concept is where we must begin in order to understand the transformation necessary to become an MSP.

The irony of the managed services industry today is that it is made up of so many companies that still have vestiges of their former break/fix selves.[8] In truth, a majority of these companies are in the process of transforming their business

---

8 The use of the term break/fix in this book is used to describe any provider engaged in delivering reactive IT services.

models.[9] This mass evolutionary process is something all IT providers must undergo if they wish to remain relevant in the IT management industry. After having spoken to thousands of companies over the years it is clear that most IT providers understand the need for this metamorphosis. Whether they are being asked by their clients for more proactive services or it is simply peer pressure from the rest of the IT channel, providers all around the world are responding to this evolutionary call.

The pull towards managed services may be strong but there is no guarantee of success. The innate DNA of break/fix companies is difficult to change. The many years of doing things a certain way makes for a hard habit to break. A relative shortage of successful role models to emulate is another reason for the many hardships today's IT provider faces while transitioning to a managed services model. However, as more and more companies become successful MSPs the more guidance they can provide to their less mature colleagues.

This brings up another important topic of discussion which deals more with a company's reluctance to take guidance from a so-called competitor than it does with their general ability to take advice. Many young MSPs have found it difficult to take advice from fellow MSPs when they view those very companies as potential competitors. This is an area of great distinction between the MSPs and other IT service providers. MSPs tend to educate themselves rather than rely on outside consultants to provide training and guidance. This practice is difficult to understand for many reactive IT providers as it marks a dra-

---

9 However, if pressed on the issue it would not be unreasonable to expect that a majority of these companies look more like break/fix, reactive IT shops than they look like mature MSPs.

matic departure from the way they have previously conducted business. Because of the unique complexities involved in creating and running a managed services practice most MSPs rely on advice from their fellow colleagues as these are the only people who truly understand their profession. As many young MSPs enter the profession they tend to look at their colleagues as competitors and therefore do not look at them as worthwhile or trustworthy sources of information.

One only need look at the legal and medical professions in order to understand how they rely on one another for information, professional advancement, and general support. Doctors and lawyers understand that the only people who can truly understand what they are going through on a day-to-day basis are other doctors and lawyers. Rather than view each other as competitors they tend to view one another as colleagues with specific areas of expertise which also strengthens and encourages the practice of referrals. For this reason, young MSPs must understand that their best (and typically only) sources of reliable information about the managed services profession are in fact other MSPs.

Realizing that being an MSP is in fact different from being a break/fix IT provider is something that few understand. Technical ability has been the most valued characteristic of IT providers for the last couple of decades. And while technical expertise is still a necessary component for MSPs it is not enough to be successful in managed services. Break/fix companies need to understand this in order to begin their transformation. Some of the most miserable failures in managed services have been break/fix companies who underestimated the non-technical changes that needed to be made. These are companies that not only did not make it as MSPs but invested large sums of money and spent a lot of time only to experience less than stellar results. In the worst scenarios these companies actually blame the business model or the technologies they purchased in an attempt to assign blame anywhere other than where it belongs. These are the companies that MSPs fear the most; companies that try, fail, and then blame.

Believe it or not, real MSPs do not fear more competition. They embrace it as more companies entering the profession can only mean more legitimacy and more business. Failed MSPs, on the other hand, only mean more dissatisfied clients and increased difficulty in convincing consumers of the importance and credibility of the managed services profession. Again, other professions do not fear increased competition as much as they fear those practitioners who are unqualified to participate in the industry. This is why most MSPs strive to ensure high standards of quality in order to prevent those who are unqualified from entering the managed services profession.

This is as good a time as any to inject a dose of optimism for any break/fix companies reading this book who may be losing hope. If you realize that your technical talent is not enough you have already taken an important first step in your transition towards the managed services profession. You must strive to break free of your former self and accept that being an

MSP is very different from the type of company you used to be. Beginning a managed services practice is not just buying some remote management tools and hanging out your shingle. Being an MSP is about providing your clients with expertise on how to make their technology serve their business interests. Most break/fix providers are unable to render that type of advice. Even if they were, their methodologies for delivering proactive IT services to their clients are not capable of maintaining a healthy and secure IT infrastructure.

What this means is that you must understand your clients' business models implicitly. Only by understanding how your clients run their businesses can you hope to understand how IT should function in that environment. It is because of this need for both technical and business acumen that many MSPs decide to specialize, either in a particular service delivery or in a market vertical.

Breaking free of the break/fix, reactive IT management culture is admittedly not easy. One need only look at the number of delusional companies out there who actually believe that they can be a break/fix MSP. This is simply not possible. What this stems from is the inability of many companies to successfully transition into managed services so they concoct this notion that they can be a reactive IT shop that is also an MSP. For these companies, self delusion is better than facing the cold reality.

No matter how you choose to accomplish this task, if you are a reactive IT service provider you must find a way to eliminate this practice in order to become an MSP. In my opinion, the easiest way to do this is to make a quick break. Reactive break/fix IT services and proactive managed services are two competing business models. These two models cannot co-exist long within the same company. Executives who think they can successfully carry on both at the same time are operating on borrowed time for it is only a matter of time before one or the other will eventually beat the other into submission.

In closing, I remain firmly convinced that the first and possibly most important step in becoming an MSP is the realization that you are becoming a different type of service provider. If you can accomplish this goal you can accomplish anything.

WHAT'S YOUR PLAN?

Break/fix companies invariably ask the question "What should I do first if I want to become an MSP?" My answer always surprises them. "Do you have an updated business plan?" "Do you have a business plan at all?" A look of genuine incredulity usually crosses their face when asked about this simple yet fundamental component of starting any new business venture. For that matter, having an up to date business plan is critical for ongoing businesses to maintain order and cohesion in whatever it is they do. I do know what these companies are asking for; it tends to be a list of the various vendor tools and a breakdown of which ones are the best. However, it is impossible to answer that question accurately without understanding more about the company that will be using those tools.

The fact that most companies wanting to enter the MSP profession do not have a business plan or any real concept of what they think their practice is going to involve should not be a surprise to anyone. One need only look at a gathering of young MSPs (or VARs) and listen to their conversations to understand that becoming an MSP is not as easy as some would make it out to be. The rewards of being an MSP are tremendous. This part is true. But most things in life that are worth something do not come for free. This is especially true with managed services.

As we have previously discussed, managed services is not a product. It is not the latest line of servers or firewalls. There is no spec sheet to hand out to sales reps that must be memorized and regurgitated by rote to customers. The decision to begin a managed services practice should never be taken lightly. But once that decision has been made one of the first steps should be to plan out the course of action for the MSP.

There are many similarities between managed services and the medical, legal, accounting, and other professions. These professions, while you may think their scope of practice is somewhat limited, do need to organize their business strategies in order to succeed. Doctors and lawyers all have plans when they begin practicing their profession. MSPs must think the same way.

Becoming an MSP should play to the strengths of the company. If a break/fix company has a particular strength in financial services then it might make sense to continue dealing with that market vertical. If your company has a lot of security experience then perhaps building some form of managed security services would be a sound plan. Some MSPs have very deep roots within a geographic community. Becoming a nationwide or international provider may not make the most sense for this type of MSP.

All this is to make the point that there are many varieties of managed services and a correspondingly wide variety of MSP. To enter this profession without having put any thought into what type of services you will offer, the clientele to whom you will offer the services, or your geographic boundaries, leaves too much to chance. Having an up to date business plan will assist you in organizing your resources to optimal effect.

Market research is fairly easy to perform and need not consume either a great amount of time or resources. You can start by examining your existing client base. A well crafted survey can provide an MSP with a lot of valuable information. If you are just starting up a new company then begin by researching the types of services or clients you wish to have. For example, if you are interested in the financial services industry then brushing up on federal banking legislation might be a good place to start. It might also be wise to understand what types of services banks typically consume. This will assist you in developing the services you will need to offer. If you plan on doing business in

London then it might be important to understand the cultural differences of doing business in that region.

No matter if you write a formal business plan or you simply scratch some notes together on the back of a napkin, formulating a plan is essential to success in managed services. Even if you are an existing company with decades of experience in the IT industry you must chart your new course towards a managed services practice by having a plan. Today, more than ever, there are new MSPs being born around the world. Each MSP is different. Having done the appropriate research and planning is critical to entering the managed services profession.

THE ROLE OF THE EXECUTIVE

It may seem to some of you rudimentary or even beneath you to read this next section, especially those readers who are executives or business owners of their companies. I strongly encourage you to fight whatever pride you may have and read this section. In fact, rip it out of this book and keep it with you at all times as a quick reference guide whenever you doubt the choices you have made in the past.

First, the bad news: more MSP firms have been ruined by lack of proper executive involvement than any other reason. Now, the good news: this problem is an easy one to fix. I have personally met with far too many companies (at various stages in their managed services transformation) only to encounter an executive staff that is incredulous as to why managed services did not pan out for them. After a few well chosen questions it is easy to understand why things did not work out.

I would have to say that lack of executive involvement ranks up there among the top reasons why companies do not successfully start a managed services practice. In some cases the idea of managed services is initiated by a mid-level technician (in really small companies this might be the business owner). Even when the executive or business owner displays initial enthusiasm in the managed services concept it generally does not last long. When an executive (especially in a larger company) ceases to remain involved in the transition process success is very difficult to achieve. The reason for this lack of involvement, as we have previously examined, tends to be the executive's belief that managed services is simply a technical challenge that must be solved. Naturally, executives in these situations will delegate this task to their director of IT or some other technical person with very little ongoing guidance or support. The technical person may come up with a list of service enabling technologies that must be acquired; they may even develop a process for delivering managed services. The business development person may come up with a marketing and sales strategy, perhaps even a plan for transitioning the existing clients over to a managed services offering. What is missing in both of these scenarios is any cohesive, long term strategy that guides all of the corporate resources towards a common goal.

Executives, even owners of small companies, must organize and execute on a variety of fronts, including technical, sales, marketing, human resources, and even legal. No one person can achieve this task alone. It must be a team effort; but a team effort with a leader. Once the executive has pledged their support for the managed services transformation process, they must stay involved. This mean, it is not enough to make the decision, delegate authority and tasks to team leaders, and then disappear from the equation. Constant attention is needed, especially during the early transformation stages. Executives must stay in touch with their team leaders so they can have regular progress reports and make any necessary adjustments to the company's managed services strategy.

Whatever your role in your company, chances are you have an important function when it comes to delivering professional grade managed services. All the parts of a corporation must be operating at efficient levels in order to ensure managed services success. This will only happen when the executive leadership has become involved and plans on staying involved all through-out the transformation process. When this happens success in managed services comes a lot more easily.

MYTH AND REALITY

There are many misconceptions about managed services in the IT channel these days. While rumors and myths are to be expected, there are some rumors and some myths that can have a deleterious effect on those MSPs who have honest inten-tions. How these rumors got started is a fascinating story but not something this book will address. We will cover many of the more common and harmful rumors and attempt to correct them as continued belief that these myths are true is something that will be harmful to the growth of the managed services profession.

Many of the following beliefs came about through sheer ignorance. Over the years, there have been many self-proclaimed experts in the field of managed services who were neither expert nor qualified to render any type of professional advice on the subject. It is my personal opinion that many of the falsehoods propagated in managed services have come from people who were not even involved in the industry. Most of these people were consultants, analysts, and members of the press. For a long time these individuals were the primary sources of information and analysis regarding the managed services profession. Today, the pendulum has swung the other way where managed services professionals are primarily responsible for information and analysis. As a result of this shift, many of these myths are being corrected.

But I already have the tools

Not a week goes by that I don't get contacted by someone asking for advice on how to get into managed services. After a few minutes they make the inevitable statement, "I just bought an MSP platform tool. Now what do I do?" This all too familiar scenario reminds me of an eager prospector with their shiny new shovel, pick axe, boots, and other gear, eager to strike it rich during the gold rush days. Eagerness is a valuable characteristic but it is not the only one you will need in order to become successful.

As we have discussed, becoming an MSP is much more than buying a tool. Unless you are willing and capable of building the technology yourself (which is almost never a recommended strategy) buying the right tools is essential to your managed services success. Ten years ago the service enabling tools were very limited and very expensive. Today, new MSP enabling technology vendors are being created every day. Lower prices, greater functionality, and better support, are just a few of the perks MSPs enjoy today.

Even with all this opportunity, selecting the correct vendor tool is essential to being a successful MSP. The myth, in case you have not figured it out yet, is that buying a tool makes you an MSP. This is no truer if you bought a pen and expected to be a Pulitzer Prize winning writer. The pen, in this example, is nothing more than an implement; something a writer uses in their craft. A hammer is a tool that is used by a carpenter to build something. In the hands of a novice, a pen or hammer is useless. The pen is merely something with which you scribble on paper and the hammer is something with which you can hit a nail. The same is true with remote monitoring and management technologies. A VAR who buys these technologies does not automatically become an MSP. The VAR must know how to put the technology to use in order to be called an MSP.

It is also worth pointing out that the entire tool selection process will go much more smoothly when the MSP has conducted the proper research and planning. I run across too many companies who buy the tool first and then try to figure out how they are going to use it. In these situations, the MSP ends up being forced into a business dictated not by their needs but by the confines of the tool they purchased.

Buying the right tools can only come when the company has conducted the appropriate research, developed an action plan, and is ready to begin deliver managed services according to their service delivery process. In these situations, the company will know precisely what tools they will need and how they will be used. I have actually come across numerous situations where the company bought MSP enabling tools but were unsure of how to use them. In some cases, the tools were fully purchased but were never installed because the company did not have any idea of how they should be used. These companies were victims of shrewd vendor salespeople, nothing more. Had these fledgling MSPs planned more they would not only have put their tools to use immediately but they would have been better prepared to research and negotiate with their vendors.

It may not be completely fair to make such a characterization but there have been numerous instances of young MSPs buying tools before they were ready. A comparable analogy might be a car dealership selling a car to someone who cannot even drive yet. In the end, we must all be responsible for our own actions and the companies buying these tools prematurely can only blame themselves. The companies that buy these tools, experience difficulty in using them, then complain that managed services is not all it is cracked up to be are the companies that do the most damage to this profession. Whether they were simply victims of unscrupulous vendor sales people is the subject of another book. However, companies would be much better prepared to deal with vendor sales reps if they had some semblance of an idea of how they were going to use the tools they were buying.

When you read these words they may seem very simplistic. This concept may seem completely logical to you. Yet, there are many companies out there buying tools and hoping that their managed services skills will soon follow. Now, if you go out and buy the shiniest, most expensive MSP enabling tool available that is completely up to you. As long as you realize that the tools will not bring experience with them. Experience, knowledge, professionalism; these things only come with time and hard work. Keep that in mind and you will be ok.

But My Clients Like Seeing Me

It never ceases to amaze how entrenched some companies are in the old ways of doing things. Even when all around them is changing, the innate urge to resist change can indeed be powerful. But when change is for the better then the reasons to resist it become less persuasive.

In particular, many reactive IT service providers will blame the lack of customer interaction on why they have not been successful in managed services. This myth is usually built around the misconception that clients actually like to see their IT service provider. The link between a client seeing a provider and experiencing an increase in IT performance may be true. However, clients also know the sensation of financial loss when they see their reactive IT provider. Even if clients like to see their provider this is no excuse to stop progress.

This myth is based upon the falsehood that clients must physically see the IT provider in order to perceive a value in the services being rendered. I suppose if remote IT management was being delivered back in the 18th century then people might actually believe that it is something of an illusion. But, we are in the 21st century and remote monitoring and management technologies are quite real. When the MSP says that their clients need to see them that tells me that the MSP does not know how to explain what it is they do. If clients knew what their MSPs were doing the client would never want to see their MSP doing work on site (except in rare situations).

Most clients, if given the appropriate information, would easily understand the concept of remote monitoring and management. Part of being an effective MSP involves educating your clients on how this new technology works. Presumably your clients have already bought into the concept of remote IT management so they must already understand the basics. Chances are, if you have done a good job of explaining managed services to your clients they will know you are doing your job even though they do not see technicians showing up in person.

Where clients really need help is in the area of differentiating managed services from reactive IT management. If clients really understood this concept they would never want to see their MSPs on-site again. It is curious, upon further reflection, that nearly all the individuals who have voiced the concern of not seeing IT providers on –site are the providers themselves and not the clients. I believe this is because the clients do not see this as a problem. This reluctance to shift towards a remote monitoring and management model is probably more fear on the part of the MSP than the client. In fact, if pressed I would not be surprised if most clients were very happy with this shift in IT management policy.

While it is a growing trend to deliver IT services (both reactive and proactive) via remote technologies, clients still need to receive assurances about the efficacy of the services they are buying. Effective reporting is a must for MSPs to communicate with their clients. In most of the cases where the MSP claims that their clients do not want to do away with on-site services the MSP has probably not considered how regular reporting and review mechanisms can help clients understand just how valuable their MSP really is. However you accomplish it education of your client should be top priority.

But I like Driving

Similar to the myth we just discussed, the following phenomenon is something that has been uttered by far too many companies (especially those who call themselves MSPs). The statement is usually uttered by field service technicians but has also been known to be made by business owners and executives. Most field technicians are creatures of habit (aren't we all) and nothing is more difficult to break than years of getting into a vehicle and driving to see your clients. When confronted with the alternative to what is commonly referred to as "truck rolls" most reactive companies claim that an onsite visit is still the most effective way of fixing the problem. They would be correct if reactive IT management was the best method available. What do I mean by that statement?

In a reactive IT management model customers will traditionally experience the problem first and then notify the provider that something is wrong and needs to be fixed. Naturally, at this point the customer only wants the problem to be fixed and the value they perceive will only be accentuated if they see someone physically at the scene performing their technical wizardry. Simple technician utilization is the name of the game here. A reactive service provider needs to have as many of their technicians billing for their services as possible in order to be profitable. Years of habit have allowed many smaller reactive shops to thrive as their business model was based on simple arithmetic. Add up how many billable hours you had, multiply times your going rate and you had your gross revenues. As a business owner, all you had to do was make sure your technicians were billing for their time as often as they could. Going on site was the natural method for delivering services under this model.

Understanding why your field technicians may be telling you that they need to go onsite is actually very important. For the most part, the simple answer is autonomy. Field technicians like being independent and autonomous from the rest of the company. At least this has been my experience in interviewing young MSPs. Particularly in larger MSPs, field technicians tend to be the heroes to their clients and the breadwinners for their employers. Typically the client will view these individuals as saviors when they arrive on site and begin working their craft. What often happens is the technician will stay on site even after the original problem has been solved because users will take advantage of their presence on scene. Because of this position, many executives are fearful of pulling these rainmakers out of the field and into the office. Part of this fear is the perceived risk of losing the client. The executive may believe that the client will no longer see a value in the company if the field technicians are no longer interacting with the client on site. The other reason executives fear reining in the field technicians is the belief that they will not be happy in their new position.

It is my belief that executives should be more forceful with their field technicians when it comes to telling them that a managed services practice does not rely on them being out of the office all the time. Field technicians must understand their role in the practice and accept that role. A managed services practice depends on the company's ability to deliver scalable and effective managed services. There are only two ways you can do this. One, you have a datacenter and deliver your managed services strictly to your clients by having their infrastructure in your facility. The second method is where you deliver remote managed services from a central location to all your clients wherever they may be.

Under a proactive IT management model scalability is essential. The only way you can make money in managed services is to leverage technology so that your technicians can scale in a way that could never be achieved under a reactive model. The truck roll can only get in the way of an MSP's hopes for achieving scalability. Only in the direst of situations should MSPs send a technician out to a client site. This will allow an MSP to centralize their service delivery operations thereby achieving greater scalability and ultimately higher profit margins.

Remote = Managed Services

Continuing on the theme of delivering services remotely, many self proclaimed MSPs have stated that because they own remote monitoring/management technologies they are delivering managed services. Again, this misconception may or may not be a product of wishful thinking on the part of the provider. Whatever the origin, self delusional or otherwise, simply having the capacity to deliver remote monitoring and remote management does not make you an MSP.

There are countless service providers today who are providing reactive IT management using their remote technologies. The fact that they employ remote management technology does not mean that they are providing proactive IT services. This brings us to potentially the most controversial statement of the book: it is impossible to deliver reactive managed services.

If you think about it, the genesis of the managed services revolution was the transition away from reactive IT management. Having remote management technology is, one could successfully argue, mandatory for any company hoping to deliver managed services. Imagine if every time you had a monitoring alert you had to dispatch someone on site to troubleshoot and fix the problem. Your profit margins would vanish almost as fast as your client base. Now put yourself in the shoes of your client. If you had to wait for someone to drive out to your location just to fix a known problem you would get fed up with such inefficient business practices.

Where this myth gets somewhat tricky is when a provider brandishes their remote management technology as proof positive that they are in fact delivering proactive managed services. Remember the pen analogy? Without an effective service delivery process, even the most powerful remote technology will not help. So the next time you hear one of your colleagues talking about their remote management tools ask them if they are delivering proactive or reactive IT management. If they cannot answer the question then chances are they are only a reactive IT shop hoping to be an MSP one day.

I'll Have One Order of Process to Go, Please

The concept of delivering remote managed services is not difficult to comprehend. Nor is the concept of delivering proactive IT services. But tell an MSP that they need to create their own service delivery process and their head will likely spin. I am not sure why this part of the transition scares so many but it is a completely needless fear. While there will be more on the topic of creating a service delivery process the main point in this section is that the process cannot be pre-packaged and sold. That would be akin to buying a personality; this is just something that each one of us has and is unique. There is no substitute for something that is so unique and personal to an individual or organization.

There are individuals today, primarily consultants, who are selling pre-packaged managed services templates that promise to help companies become MSPs instantly. These overnight transformation solutions are generally more hype than substance as I have never seen a true MSP that was built overnight. To the extent that they promise to deliver a ready to go service delivery process these kits ought to be viewed with a healthy dose of skepticism.

A service delivery process is something that not only is unique to each MSP but the creation of this process is something that every MSP should undergo. Part of the experience medical and legal students go through during school is the process of learning how to think like a doctor or lawyer. All the books and study aids cannot short cut the process of training a mind how to think. It is the journey of doing the work yourself that makes the individual a professional. Similarly, an MSP must go through the journey of creating a service delivery process in order to truly understand how they will be delivering their managed services. Attempts to cut corners or circumvent this necessary and important part of an MSP's training are only doing harm to the MSP. In the end, the MSP will only be cheating themselves and their clients if they believe that they can borrow someone else's service delivery process and use it as their own.

Template SLAs

I must issue a disclaimer before proceeding with this next section. Yes, my legal training does shape many of the issues about which I write and talk. In law school I spent countless hours reading about how companies would get into very sticky and costly arguments. Often, the entire dispute could have been prevented had the parties taken rather simple precautions at the outset of their relationship. Service Level Agreements are one area where I believe the managed services profession will have a rude awakening in the near future.

SLA's have become a hot topic of conversation between MSPs and there is nothing more saddening than seeing a lot of well intending MSPs risk their entire business on such a foolish thing as a template SLA. In their defense, most MSPs have not had to deal with legal issues of the sort they have to deal with today. For many new MSPs, regulatory compliance and legal liability are new concepts. But, as every law student knows all too well: ignorance of the law is no defense.

Template SLAs started making their way around the MSP community a few years back. Some of these documents were offshoots from the hosting industry while others were given to MSPs by their vendors. Whatever their origins, template SLAs can leave an MSP business exposed in many ways that are unknown to the company. Because each MSP is unique, the type of legal document they use should also be unique. As has been previously stated, you could take 10 MSPs all using the same technology and serving the same client base and come up with 10 different business models. Naturally, those 10 MSPs would also need 10 different SLAs to codify their agreements with clients.

Some MSPs believe, mistakenly, that because they are engaged in the same profession that they can borrow and use another company's SLA for their own. While fear (or dislike) of attorneys and the presumed cost of engaging one to draft an SLA may be the root cause of this belief, the cost of losing a court battle due to a poorly worded SLA is simply not worth the risk. Taking another company's SLA, replacing their name with yours is not a sound legal practice much less a sound business practice. This is like you asking your friend for their last will and testament, scratching out their name and inserting your own. Would you leave your family at the mercy of a document that was written for someone else? You probably would not. Then why would you leave your company in a similar situation?

There are a few simple steps that you can take to safeguard your MSP practice.

1) Talk to an attorney. Talking to your friend who has a brother who talked to an attorney is not good enough. If you work for an MSP and you are not using an SLA

that was drafted or reviewed by an attorney then you are probably at risk.

2) Each MSP is different. We have already covered how no two MSPs are alike. If you accept this premise, then you should have no problem in applying it to SLAs. More importantly, you should view your SLA in the same way as you prepared for beginning your managed services practice. The types of clients you have, the types of services you offer, the location of you and your clients, and many other factors will enter your SLA making that document as unique as your business.

3) Watch out for phonies. There a lot of people out there dispensing advice on managed services today. Be mindful of those who would tell you how to draft your SLA. If they are not a legal professional then take their advice with a grain of salt. Tell your attorney about the advice you received and then if they feel it is good advice they can include it in your SLA. Otherwise, trust a trained legal professional when it comes to the drafting of your legal documents.

Remember that an SLA is a contract; an agreement between two or more parties. Your contracts should be drafted, and at the very least reviewed, by a trained legal professional who can render advice on how best to codify your company's intentions. As the managed services industry becomes more regulated having a well constructed SLA will become essential for every MSP.

Managed services and hardware don't mix

The advent of managed services caused many in the IT channel to believe, mistakenly, that MSPs would stop selling hardware to their clients. This belief has been one of the most damaging falsehoods in the managed services industry because of the detrimental effect it has had on the relationship between service providers and vendors. While this misconception has largely been corrected in recent years it is difficult to accurately detail the damage that it has caused to MSPs everywhere.

The origin of the belief that MSPs do not sell hardware is difficult to pinpoint but the reason behind the belief being created is not. We have discussed how the shrinking margins of VARs and system integrators began the managed services revolution. These companies were heavily dependent on product sales to drive revenues. After the dotcom crash the combination of shrinking IT budgets along with increased competition from large hardware distributors made the longstanding VAR business model extremely undesirable and unsustainable. Many companies during this time period were acquired or simply ceased operations as a result of their inability to adapt to the changing business trends. It is likely around this time period that certain people began to divorce the concept of hardware sales from managed services.

As time went on and the managed services profession continued to build momentum the idea that these MSPs were not selling hardware like their VAR counterparts also built momentum. Although it was never enunciated formally there were subtle tones and passing comments made in many of the major technical trade magazines referencing the differences between MSPs and VARs. These subtle, passing comments over time painted a picture of both ignorance and sometimes contempt for the managed services profession.

Today, with the gift of hindsight, it is easy to divine a meaning in all these signs and come to a fairly accurate understanding of why these writers and pundits thought the way they did.[10] Once again, the simple fundamentals of economics can often lead the astute observer to the hidden yet easily discoverable truth. In the early years of managed services many writers, analysts, and consultants believed that anything that got in the way of hardware sales would be an inconvenience that could not be tolerated. But why is this so?

For many years hardware vendors have been the primary benefactors to the gigantic business machine that is the IT channel. Product vendors pay for advertising, sponsorships and exhibitions, consulting, research, and anything else that will help them understand and sell to the IT channel. This ecosystem fuels the IT channel in many positive ways. Vendors get to showcase their wares while the VARs are educated about new technologies.

Many IT channel magazine publishers believe that this important business must not be disrupted and must be protected at all costs. At least that's what the power brokers believed.

10 Today there are relatively few who believe that MSPs do not influence or sell hardware.

And they were correct. This is a relatively good system. The problem began when these individuals in positions of influence and power started dismissing the managed services profession as unimportant. I am not saying that people have to like managed services; I'm sure there are those out there who do not. However, what is intolerable to me, as well as many thousands of MSPs, is the notion that members of the press, analyst, and consulting communities would intentionally pervert and distort the managed services profession in order to preserve the industry of technology hardware and software.

As should be quite evident by now MSPs actually have a great deal of influence when it comes to the technologies their clients purchase. For years MSPs have been leveraging their trusted advisor status to assist their clients with which technologies they should buy. This important relationship has irrevocably changed the way hardware and software is purchased. What confused many in the IT channel was the change in how MSPs conducted business versus how VARs conducted business. MSPs, rather than buy and resell products, tend to advise their clients on which products they should buy. VARs had this same practice but with one major difference. VARs never had to consider how that hardware would be supported and maintained in the long term. Of course a VAR would never dream of selling poorly constructed equipment that would ultimately breakdown. This would never serve the VAR's interests. However, there is a difference between reselling and managing hardware. MSPs must manage that which they sell. MSPs will be responsible for ensuring that the hardware their clients buy work as they should work.

As we will examine later on the concept of Hardware as a Service is revolutionizing how MSPs provide their services. For now, it should be clear that MSPs do in fact rely heavily on hardware to perform their duties. This practice has changed little from when these same MSPs were VARs. What has changed is how the hardware is procured.

TEACHING OLD CLIENTS NEW TRICKS

A commonly voiced concern by companies entering the managed services profession[11] is what to do with the existing clients. More specifically, the issue is how to transition existing clients into managed services clients without impacting the company's cash flow in a negative way. This problem has been encountered by countless new MSPs and in some cases it has prompted these companies to abandon their practice altogether.

This need not be a problem with proper planning and execution. A variety of client transition models have been employed throughout the years with varying degrees of success. We will discuss several of the more popular methods and illustrate how they can be used to create a smooth transition. It must be noted that success in this process depends almost entirely on the ability of the company to execute. Even the most well constructed plans can suffer from a lack of proper execution. This is why

11 This problem is not an issue with startup MSPs.

the executives in the company must be involved, preferably setting the corporate objectives when it comes to managed services. There is really no way to determine which is going to be the best model for transitioning clients to a managed services offering but you can minimize risk through adequate planning.

The Fast Track to Managed Services

One model that is commonly used is the "rip the band aid" scenario where the company forces its clients into a managed services offering by refusing to offer other reactive IT management services. The name (which is unofficial) comes from the MSP deciding to change their service offerings almost immediately with little or no client transition period. One benefit of this approach is that the company will know very quickly how many of its existing clients will be purchasing managed services. Companies with a large base of existing clients tend to be more conservative in their migration plans but this model can be used to great effect by those companies who are sure about their managed services objectives.

Fear of a decrease in revenues is a natural feeling for companies in the transition process. While this fear is quite normal, companies who have a solid belief that managed services is the right thing for them tend to embrace this model as it gets them out of the reactive IT management business very quickly. For these types of companies managed services represents the only legitimate form of IT management. A properly planned and executed strategy for entering the managed services profession leaves no room for retreat. They view reactive IT management as an outdated and inferior practice and refuse to subject their clients to such inefficiencies. By preventing the sales and marketing teams from selling it and refusing to allow the technical team to deliver such a service, the company can very effectively guide its existing clients into a new and better form of IT management.

Other companies do not see things in such a black and white manner. The decision to enter the profession of managed services can be very easy for many companies. The pressure from competitors, vendors, and even clients can be overwhelming. The managed services message is ubiquitous in the channel and has been for the past few years. Even with all this momentum towards managed services it is often difficult to go to a client and tell them that the way you do business with them will change.

Naturally, a certain amount of time must be accounted for when asking clients to transition to managed services. However, the approach of making this transition as quick as possible has found a legitimate place within the managed services industry.

The Moderated Approach

This brings us to the next model for transition, which also happens to be the model most commonly employed. While it is not something easy to define or label, the model can best be described as a moderated approach where the company offers both reactive and proactive forms of IT services to its client base. Seen as a more cautious approach to entering managed services many companies who use this model tend to produce a lengthier and drawn out transition period along with greater feelings of dissatisfaction by the company.

Some of you may view this transition strategy as a safe route into managed services, and you would be correct if the strategy was executed properly. However, more often than not, this strategy does not work or if it does it takes a long time to produce any meaningful results. Why is this? Particularly with VARs, integrators, and other reactive service providers, the sales, marketing, and technical staff tend to revert back to what they know best when faced with the challenge of selling and delivering managed services. Companies can display all the outward appearances of being in managed services, including the appropriate terminology on their website and marketing collateral and having the necessary technical equipment. Yet, upon close examination the company cannot produce any real results. They have very few managed services clients and their pipeline is anemic at best.

This cautious model does appear very tempting to those companies who have been in business for many years and do not wish to take any significant risks at this stage in their careers; a very natural and sympathetic position in which to be. However, this temptation may not be worth it in the end. Companies who adopt this model must be cautious not to end up like so many of their colleagues. These companies have a few managed services clients but are never able to completely leave the old ways behind them as they have too many reactive clients demanding too many resources to allow the managed services to thrive. They have, as I have often referred to it, one foot in each boat. This is a very precarious position to be in as it risks both the managed services and reactive sides of the business.

The best companies in the world do one thing very well (at least the good ones start off this way). A company rarely achieves success by being many things to many people. Have you ever wondered why other professions refer so much business to their colleagues? They know that attempting something that is beyond their area of expertise only harms their professional reputation. I have seen far too many MSPs who have deluded themselves into thinking that they were on the road to success when in fact they were being hindered by their reactive side of the business.

A good MSP will see their reactive clients for what they truly are; a deterrent from expanding further into managed services. Yes, eliminating these clients can mean a loss in revenue. But when you examine the data closely, you will see that having $1000 in reactive revenue may not necessarily be the same as having $1000 in managed services revenue. A well run MSP should be able to make at least 40% gross profit margins without breaking a sweat. Higher profit margins are a product of a lower cost of delivering services. Higher gross profit margins also equate into higher corporate valuations when it comes time to sell the company.

There must be a time when every MSP decides that its reactive clients are nothing more than dead weight in the path of progress. A troubled or inexperienced company may never want to lose that revenue. A more seasoned company will muster the courage to fire those clients when they are not in alignment with the company's objectives. This is just good business sense.

Creating a New Company

For some businesses, starting fresh is sometimes the best course of action. There have been several good examples of companies who have started separate business units just for managed services. Some have created separate divisions that share some resources with the reactive or "other" side of the house while others have opted to go even further by creating a completely separate legal entity just for managed services. Depending on how it is executed, this model can be quite effective. It also represents one of the more serious transition processes.

Creating a separate division can be a fairly straight forward process for many companies, especially smaller ones. Through up a new website, create some marketing collateral, invest in the infrastructure, and you are all set. Where it gets tricky is when the company plays favorites by pitting the MSP side against the other. This is particularly troublesome when the reactive side of the house has advantages that the MSP side does not enjoy.

For example, there was a company that had been in business for many years as a successful VAR. They had a solid reputation in their region and had plenty of goodwill and technical expertise on which to build their managed services offering. After creating their go to market plan they opted for creating a separate division of their company. This new division was to be housed in the same building as the reactive side and would share some of the same staff as well. A new name, website, and marketing presence were to be created in order to complete the creation of this new entity. This model helped the company begin its managed services practice by segregating the existing reactive operations from the new managed services operations.

There is a tremendous benefit in keeping a new managed services practice from the old side of the business. It prevents distraction and minimizes the potential for the new managed services clients to be scavenged by the reactive sales and marketing team. Too often a new managed services offshoot will come under attack by break/fix and reactive IT personnel. This is very common when the executives have failed to erect proper barriers between the two divisions. As oftentimes occurs, the executives will believe that a lead is a lead and simply throw it into the sales funnel for the reactive and managed services teams to fight over. Because the managed services side of the business is new and usually under funded, they usually end up with the short end of the stick.

In order to achieve the most from your new managed services endeavor, you need to allocate the appropriate amount of resources, which includes marketing and lead generation. Creating a new division only to let the old side of the business clip its wings does not make any sense. Plus, it is a huge waste of resources.

The second way is to create an entirely new MSP business entity. This model relies on complete segregation from any existing business other than perhaps a common set of owners or investors. The executives and staff are usually dedicated solely to running it, there is no competition from any other division, and it is funded adequately. Under these conditions, the MSP actually has a very good chance of succeeding. One example of such a strategy was another VAR that created a new MSP company with the objective of growing it until it could sustain itself as a going concern. Once it did achieve that goal, the MSP was merged back into the company where it currently resides today. The lesson to be learned here is that the MSP "experiment" was conducted in an environment where there was no risk of the VAR side taking advantage of the managed services side. Having its own sales and marketing team is very important to ensuring the success of any new MSP division or company.

Whichever model you choose, in order for it to work, your managed services practice must be allowed to play on equal footing with the other business divisions of the company. If you also have a VAR or integrator division do not let those sales people have access to managed services leads as they will sell them on anything and everything except managed services. Remember, the objective of this new division or company should be to become a viable managed services practice that can operate on its own. Whether the MSP division or company is merged back into the company is up to you. But, starting a new company or division specifically to offer managed services displays a company's sincerest efforts to enter this profession.

How you transition your company into a managed services practice can never be made into a cookie cutter process. Just like each MSP being unique from the other, the same is true with the various paths available for transitioning from reactive to proactive IT management. Whichever path you choose, make sure it is a well considered plan that is designed to get you to a point of sustainable managed services revenue as quickly as possible.

SELLING MANAGED SERVICES

Depending on who you talk to there are some in the managed services profession who believe it is impossible to "sell" managed services. That is to say they believe you cannot sell managed services in the same way a VAR sells products. After having watched this industry for so many years, I would have to agree with this statement. One thing is for certain, selling managed services is vastly different from selling other IT products and services. In this section we will examine some of the more effective theories and practices for selling and marketing a managed service.

Once again, a disclaimer must be issued. The general topic of sales and marketing has produced volumes of content and discussion over the years. The managed services industry is no exception. I have read very compelling sales books written by ex-car salesmen that are actually quite engaging, well written, and make a lot of sense. However, much of what is written in these books has very little application in the managed services universe. Having spent so much time in and among MSPs has taught me a lot. One of the things I have learned is that when it comes to sales and marketing, I do not subscribe to any of the usual motivational sales tactics used to prod and incent sales people into doing their jobs better. These tactics are simply not effective when applied to a managed services environment. Companies that have been successful in managed services have realized this important distinction. Knowing this can put your MSP at a significant advantage to your competition.

First, we must look at how managed services differ from other IT products. There are very few product sales people who can sell managed services well. In fact, there are few product sales people who can sell managed services at all. This single phenomenon can be linked to the hardships many MSPs have faced over the years as they have migrated from a reactive IT model. Once again, culture and years of habit are the culprits behind much of the inability of these product sales people to understand the value proposition of managed services. The purpose of this chapter is not to teach sales 101. Rather, our purpose here is to identify some of the more common trends and theories of selling managed services.

There will always be good salespeople and bad salespeople. In the IT businesses, good sales people are just as hard to find as good car salesmen. I am sure that there have been MSP executives who have been frustrated by their lack of success primarily due to an underperforming managed services salesperson. There is no secret trick to identifying bad salespeople. As an executive, you simply need to know that they exist and you really need to be able to spot them when they work for you.

As I explained, this chapter is not about describing industry secrets on how to sell managed services or how to create managed services sales professionals. There are just some basic characteristics that exist among all successful sales people. More importantly, there are definite limitations when it comes to what a hardware salesperson can do with a managed services offering. And while good IT product sales people may be under the impression that they are going to make a killing at selling managed services, this notion is more than likely not ever going to happen.

The best product salespeople usually follow a formula. The formula may differ from person to person but there are some commonalities. First, they all realize the important of making calls. Depending on the product they are selling, the company to whom they are selling, and several other variables, every good sales person knows roughly how many calls will yield a physical meeting. They know how many meetings will yield a second meeting. And they know how many second meetings will produce a sale. This simple algorithm can be relied upon time after time and as long as the process is followed there will be some fairly predictable results.

This predictability is where most product sales people get off on the wrong foot when they are handed a managed services offering and told to sell it to their clients. A successful product sales person will approach managed services with the same perspective as their product. Features, functionality, and price, are usually some of the more prominent tricks used by salespeople. This product will do this for you...this product processes this amount of data...this product costs 10 percent less than the others. This is how a good product salesperson will engage their prospect and hopefully lure them into believing that the product is worth buying.

This is not how you sell managed services, however. Selling managed services demands a knack for understanding how clients think. It demands an intimate knowledge of the differences between products and services. A managed services relationship is about trust; trust between the client and the MSP. Buying a product does not demand trust on the part of the client. If the product is bad or was misrepresented in any way, then there are recourses available to the consumer. Products are inherently different that way because they either work or do not work. Consumers can talk to other consumers who have used the product in question and find out all there is to know.

Services, on the other hand, cannot be returned easily. Clients buying services tend to want more than a money back guarantee. Especially when dealing with something as sensitive and IT management, clients giving over access to their IT network want to know that the MSP is qualified and trustworthy. This is what a good managed services salesperson has to sell. The reason many managed services sales people produce less than stellar results is tied to the fact that they cannot distinguish between the unique buying characteristics of managed services clients and product clients. Let's take the example of an insurance sales person.

Selling insurance is difficult. There is no physical box or widget that is transferred at the time of sale. An insurance policy is an abstract thing, one that is very hard to describe to most consumers. If you go to the store and buy a hammer for $10, this transaction is very easy to comprehend. You give the store $10 and they give you a hammer. You have something tangible when you leave the store. There is a concrete object in your hand that reminds you of why you no longer have $10 in your pocket.

A managed services contract is one of the most elusive services sold because if the MSP is doing their job correctly the client will have no problems, experience little pain, and life in general (at least as it relates to their IT performance) should be good. Explaining this benefit to the client is a difficult job. It requires knowledge about client's business, how their business operates, how they use IT, how their IT could be made better, and lots of other intangibles that require excellent communication skills on the part of the sales person. When a product sales person transitions into selling managed services they no longer have something tangible to hand over to their client. Instead, they have a concept; a better way of doing things that must be communicated to the client in such a way that trust is built between the two parties in a relatively short period of time. There is a reason some of the best managed services sales people have come from other services sales positions. They already understand these fundamentals. Services are second nature to them. True, the type of services they are selling may be different, but the underlying skills required (i.e., communication and good perception) are pretty much the same.

Another theory that has been commonplace in the managed services industry is that of marketing versus selling. Other professions operate (i.e., legal, medical, accounting, etc.) under the assumption that consumers know who they must contact when they have specific problems. For example, if you break a bone you go to a doctor. If you in legal trouble you seek out an attorney. If you need your tax returns prepared you go to an accountant. These professions do no actively sell their services. Rather, they rely upon the popular knowledge that they are experts in their chosen fields and consumers will seek them out when they are needed.

The managed services profession is not yet at the stage where consumers inherently know to seek out an MSP when they have problems with their IT. The industry is, however, making very good progress towards this level of consumer awareness. The global consumer market is aware of IT service providers but they do not yet understand the difference between proactive IT management and reactive IT management. This is where a managed services sales person must attack first. Educating clients about the benefits of proactively managing IT is critical to the mass awareness that must exist in order for managed services to stand beside other professions.

The best managed services sales people educate their clients. A good salesperson will not spend time trying to convince their prospects that they should buy managed services. Instead, a good salesperson will spend time educating them on why their IT needs to be managed and how to manage their IT. Then, when the time is right, a properly educated client will come to the conclusion that in order to properly bring their IT under control they must either do it themselves or hire an MSP. This is the basic process that must be completed in order to sell managed services. The client must be educated as to the nature of the problem and then they must trust that the MSP is the right entity for the job.

Cold calling has been a tried and true methodology for selling products but has not traditionally had any success in the managed services industry. Effective lead generation, therefore, has been a problem for many managed services sales teams as they struggle to achieve those necessary touch points with prospective clients. Since cold calling does not yield beneficial results, many sales professionals will revert back to what they know best: selling products. This problem can only be solved by proper management techniques. Financial incentives, training, and education of sales personnel are critical to producing managed services sales. Left to choose what they will sell, sales personnel will invariably go back to what is easy and effective. For this reason many MSP executives have found it particularly useful to separate product and services sales staff.[12]

Until managed services become a household name (and that day is rapidly approaching) sales people must learn how to educate their prospects on the value of managed services, as well as

---

12 This is another reason for creating a separate business entity that focuses exclusively on managed services. Doing this will separate the various sales and marketing teams preventing any chance of cannibalism, as well as, prevent any chance of the sales people reverting back to their old ways.

the relationship between MSPs and their clients. A client that understands these essentials is ready to buy managed services.

RESELLING MANAGED SERVICES

The topic of reselling managed services is very sensitive. I am aware that there will be people reading this book whose business model involves reselling someone else's managed services or offering their own managed services to resellers. During this chapter much will be said about the distinction between partnering and reselling. Part of the difficulty in writing this chapter has to do with separating (for the reader) what the reality is versus what is right or good for the industry. The only thing I can do is present the facts as best I can and let you the reader come to your own conclusions.

The purpose of this chapter is to provide the reader with an understanding of the managed services industry with regards to reselling. This chapter will help the reader better understand the pros and cons of reselling (both as a reseller and as the MSP). In addition, this chapter will delve into some of the pitfalls inherent in the managed services reseller model. No matter what your views on this topic, this chapter will hopefully serve to help you look at this subset of the managed services profession in a new and interesting light.

UNDERSTANDING THE CONCEPT OF RESELLING MANAGED SERVICES

Reselling managed services was bound to happen, especially in an industry like IT. Reselling is in the blood, the very DNA of IT companies throughout the world. Perhaps it is because of this deep history of reselling that many IT companies have found delivering their own managed services a challenge. While this process of becoming an MSP is getting easier, for many IT service providers the temptation to resell another MSPs services can be very strong. This chapter will attempt to make sense of all the angles when it comes to reselling. We will examine the benefits and negatives to this model, as well as the reasons why an MSP may or may not want to consider delivering their own services through other MSPs.

Reselling managed services is a relatively new phenomenon. If you consider that managed services has been in the mainstream for approximately 10-15 years it is only in the last 5 years that the idea of reselling managed services has been an accepted practice.

Those who can't do, teach. This saying, while not entirely fair to apply to all MSPs, does accurately describe a small but notorious group of MSPs who have decided to stop selling to end-user consumers and have begun delivering their managed services through other resellers. This practice began during the first few years of this century in response to a sluggish economy and as an overall attempt to increase revenues when consumers were not spending money.

It is not difficult to understand why this practice began. When hard times fell on these early adopters (due to economic and other factors not entirely in their control) their natural instincts were to try and find another outlet for their managed services. Nobody would begrudge a company for trying to survive in difficult conditions. However, it is worth noting that this practice was not employed by the majority of MSPs during this time period. Instead, it was a practice utilized by a few companies who were searching for alternative sources of revenues.

In the last couple of years, interest in reselling managed services has been on the rise, primarily fueled by two groups. The first have been MSPs who have more mature services offerings and may have experienced difficulty in selling managed services to their clients (this is not always the case). The second group is comprised of predominantly smaller IT shops who are interested in getting into managed services but who do not want to invest any time or resources. For them, reselling is a way to enter the industry without any significant effort. There are some strong feelings about reselling managed services and I hope that this chapter provides some food for thought, no matter where you stand on this issue.

ADVANTAGES OF RESELLING MANAGED SERVICES

The amount of interest in managed services has been increasing for the last several years at a rate that is truly staggering. Not only is the level of interest in managed services on the rise but the interest is coming from many different geographic regions. As the interest in managed services increases and as more consumers demand proactive IT management from their service providers the impatience for the time needed to get into managed services also increases. The IT channel, as we have previously discussed, is being bombarded with a common set of messages: get into managed services fast, increase recurring revenues, and obtain higher profit margins. This constant barrage of messaging is having an effect. IT providers everywhere are rapidly buying equipment, attending conferences, and learning about how to become MSPs. For some, though, the time and resources required to build a successful managed services practice is too high; they want immediate gratification.

Now, before we pass judgment, in some cases, this need for immediate transformation is legitimate. Many companies have reported a strong demand for managed services from their existing clients. This increased demand for managed services will only increase over the next 5 to 10 years. As the demand for managed services increases so will the demand for IT providers to make the transformation into managed services. This pressure on IT providers to start delivering high value managed services will inevitably cause some to consider a reseller arrangement whereby they deliver another MSP's managed services. Regardless of how late a company is in their adoption of managed services, the increasing pressure on today's IT providers is very real and quite strong.

First, let us look at the advantages to reselling managed services. The most obvious advantage is increased time to market. Especially when driven by customer demand, rather than risk losing clients due to lack of responsiveness a company can quickly deliver managed services to that client in a very short period of time. In a time when many customers have increasing choices as to who their MSP will be, IT providers do not always have time on their side. Increased time to market from reselling managed services is not just a benefit to reactive IT providers. Many MSPs can benefit from partnering with other MSPs in strategic areas.

For example, it is not uncommon for MSPs to encounter a client that demands a particular service the MSP cannot (or does not currently) deliver. In these situations, the MSP has an existing relationship with the client and does not want to see it disrupted. Several options are available to the MSP. One, they can refer the client to another MSP that specializes in that particular service. Or two, they can partner with that MSP to deliver the service to the client as if it were their own. The latter option is often chosen as it allows the MSP to satisfy the client's needs without having to give up control. This is a form of reselling[13] and it occurs often. Because of the unique relationship between MSP and client, most MSPs guard their

---

13 Although the term used here is reselling, there are many in the industry that would classify this type of relationship as more partnering than reselling.

clients very jealously. Since most MSPs cannot be all things to their clients, delivering some services via a reseller model can work to everyone's advantage.

Another major advantage to reselling managed services is in the ability to experiment without the need to invest time or resources. The sheer number of new entrants into managed services is naturally producing a lot of companies interested in but unsure of how to proceed with regards to managed services. There are many companies right now who are aware of the need to begin offering managed services but are unsure of what steps they need to take in order to become successful. For many of these companies, reselling another MSPs managed services might make sense. By partnering with another MSP a company can deliver high value managed services to their clients with very little expense or effort. This method can work very effectively, especially for those companies that are not ready to make the commitment to transform their organization.

The pressure on most IT providers today to offer managed services is considerable. At times, it must seem like a constant drumbeat of vendors, colleagues, and clients all saying the same thing. This pressure on business owners and executives cannot be dismissed. In many cases the IT providers have been in business for a long time and to expect them to change their business model overnight is asking a lot of anyone. Even those IT providers who are convinced of the need to offer managed services to their clients may feel better about a moderated approach whereby they resell as they create their own brand of managed services. This model is actually quite like the old guilds where young apprentices would be taught and guided by a more experienced professional. It was only a century ago that legal industry taught their new lawyers in much the same way.

These are but a few of the advantages to reselling another MSP's managed services. If you are interested in reselling another MSPs managed services then that is perfectly fine. As long as you understand that there are certain things which may never be circumvented or avoided simply because you are reselling someone else's services. It is natural that many candidates for reselling will be less mature and unaware of their professional obligations to their clients. Whatever your motivation for deciding to resell managed services, the choice of which MSP is obviously of paramount importance.

DISADVANTAGES OF RESELLING MANAGED SERVICES

We have examined when reselling managed services makes sense. Now we will look at when reselling managed services does not make sense. Or, at least, we will examine what it will not do for a company. Please note that this section is not meant to be an indictment of any particular business model employed by MSPs today. Rather, it is an attempt to dispel some of the more common characteristics companies attribute to the managed services reseller model.

A common misconception among IT providers is that reselling another MSPs services will provide all the benefits of being an MSP. Companies need to know the truth about reselling and what it does and does not provide. Understanding the facts about reselling managed services will help companies make the right choices when it comes to the ultimate decision of build versus partner

In order to understand what reselling managed services is not, it might be easier to first start with all the key benefits a properly designed and implemented managed services offering should produce. This way we can see which benefits exist under a managed services reseller model.

Recurring Revenues

Let us begin with recurring revenues. Most companies focus on recurring revenues as one of the principle benefits of becoming an MSP. The ability to bill a client on a regular basis for services rendered is extremely powerful to a company wanting to have reliable and contractually bound revenues. Reselling managed services can produce this benefit. As long as the service is meaningful and the client wants to continue paying for it, where the services are being delivered does not really matter.

A reseller offering managed services can enjoy the recurring revenues from this relationship. Recent theories in the managed services profession are testing the foundations of the reseller model. The recurring revenues of a managed services relationship are clear when dealing only with the MSP and the client. When you insert a reseller into the middle then things get tricky. Client ownership becomes the central issue. When a reseller decides to terminate the relationship and wishes to become an MSP themselves does the MSP or the reseller own the client relationship? The outcome of this question will dictate who receives the recurring revenues. As long as a reseller understand the risks of client ownership in this type of relationship this model can provide significant advantages.

Profit Margins

The next significant benefit of being an MSP is high profit margins. In the early days of managed services, shrinking margins from product sales as well as the uncertainty of chasing projects was enough of a reason for a company to enter the managed services profession. The same is true today. Even an average MSP should be able to yield between 30-40% gross profit margins from their managed services clients. The better MSPs will consistently extract gross margins in excess of 50% with some of the more advance MSPs hitting the 70-80% margin range. These numbers represent a very compelling reason to enter this profession.

However, there has been absolutely no data to suggest that a reseller of managed services can hope to approach these kinds of margins. The most reliable data so far seems to suggest that around 20% is the most a reseller can hope to make. The reason for this should be obvious. The MSP delivering the services will be keeping a large portion of the revenues for themselves for legitimate operating costs. This is, in fact, how an MSP should operate leaving only a fixed amount of profit margin left over for the reseller. If it is your stated objective to begin offering managed services in order to get your company into a higher bracket of profit margins then you should probably not consider reselling. Please note that a company wishing to test the market first before making a large commitment may want to try reselling first. Similarly, an existing MSP may find it expedient to partner with another MSP for a particular type of service before deciding to offer it themselves. In these and other cases reselling does and will continue to make sense. However, it is important to understand that high profit margins will only be a product of delivering your own managed services.

Customer Retention

During the days of break/fix and reactive IT management customer retention was a problem for many IT providers. Because the type of products and services delivered were not particularly high value or unique clients had an abundance of choice when it came to who they could select to design, build, and maintain their networks. Managed services changed the relationship between providers and clients. Because managed services involves such a high level of trust on the part of the client once that relationship is formed it is difficult to break. Yes there are clients who fire their MSPs in favor of another, but that is a rare occurrence. Provided the MSP is doing their job, a majority of clients will continue to rely on their MSP through thick and thin.

As a reseller of managed services, customer retention is a plausible concept. In other words, as long as the MSP is doing their job the reseller should benefit from that hard work. As a reseller the retention of your clients is ultimately decided by the MSP, and not you. If the MSP makes a mistake and negatively impacts the client then the client will naturally seek out the party with whom they are most familiar: the reseller. Customers will not care that you are not responsible for their network problems nor will they be forgiving about why you may not have told them that you were never delivering the managed services in the first place. What customers want to know is that their data and IT infrastructure are in good hands. In this regard, client retention is about the customer experience. The more parties you insert into the equation the more chance there is of one of those links breaking.

Company Valuation

The world of Mergers and Acquisitions (M&A) is a complex one. The process of buying or selling a company can be long, drawn out, and aggravating. Conversely, a well executed merger or acquisition can yield tremendous benefits to both parties involved. Many MSPs have seen their company valuations skyrocket as a result of their managed services offerings. Contractually bound recurring revenues, high profit margins, and high customer retention rates all contribute to corporate valuations that are much higher than typical reactive IT provider companies.

Many MSPs anticipate the day when they can sell their businesses. M&A multiples of one times revenues are typical for break/fix IT companies. In many M&A negotiations, any revenue that is not tied to a contract will typically be discounted to nearly nothing. The rationale behind this practice is that non-contractually bound revenue poses too much of a risk since the client can easily take their business elsewhere. Hence, buyers like to see a contract in place as security that the client will be less likely to look for a different MSP. Right or wrong, there are many reasons why the practice of discounting non-recurring revenues is commonly employed during M&A negotiations. Whatever your views on this practice are, there is no evidence to suggest that a reseller of managed services would derive the benefit of higher corporate valuations.

Under a reseller agreement the MSP delivering the managed services holds a majority of the value in the relationship. Even though the reseller may interact with the client on a more frequent basis they are still beholden to the MSP to deliver the services. Similarly, when the client has a change of needs a reseller is in a more precarious position as they must either get their MSP to offer new services or they must find another MSP with whom to partner. For this reason alone, many companies choose not to rely solely on one MSP for all their services.

WHEN TO OFFER YOUR SERVICES TO OTHER MSPS

Much of the discussion thus far has been about the advantages and disadvantages to reselling another MSPs managed services. Now, we will examine the same topic but from a different perspective. It is natural for mature MSPs to look at what they have created and think that their unique brand of managed services is good enough for another IT provider to resell. For others, difficulty in marketing and selling managed services may lead them to believe that creating a channel through which their managed services will be sold is a good way to increase revenues. Unfortunately, this is easier said than done.

Selling anything through the channel can be a difficult process that takes time and resources to fully exploit. Vendors often spend years perfecting their channel strategies and programs. For an MSP with little or no experience in selling through the channel, such an ordeal can be overwhelming. One of the first mistakes made by MSPs with channel ambitions is the confusion they create amongst their colleagues and future customers. As MSPs, other IT providers have a unique bond with their fellow colleagues. Members of the IT channel share common experiences, fight the same battles with vendors, and have the same frustrations with customers. All these commonalities vanish when an MSP becomes a vendor. As a vendor, an MSP must change their business model including their pricing, marketing, sales, and service delivery in order to meet the demands of their new clients.

MSPs who sell through the channel must also be prepared to deal with a whole host of new problems they never had to face when selling direct to the end-user. Underperforming channel partners, new pricing models, and many new challenges can confuse and hamper a company's channel ambitions. Selling managed services is difficult enough. Selling managed services through the channel is no less difficult. Many MSPs never fully anticipate the new challenges they must face when selling their managed services through the channel. They must take on new characteristics that make them more like a vendor than a service provider.

Competition with channel partners is an important issue that must be addressed by both MSP and reseller alike. Just as a reactive IT provider must transition into managed services so must an MSP also transition if they want to sell through the channel. More than one MSP has found themselves in dire straits after they have begun the process of building an MSP channel. What frequently happens is the realization that the MSP experiences shrinking revenue (as a result of a majority of their resources being focused on the channel) and an increase in their overhead costs as a result of the new demands from their channel partners. When an MSP creates a channel they are also creating a group of partners that needs almost constant attention and cultivation in order to produce any results from that partner. Sales, technical, marketing, and many other forms of training are required in order to help a channel partner become an effective managed services reseller. Just ask any of the vendors who have been in the managed services channel for any length of time and they will quickly tell you that cultivating an effective channel is not an easy task. Dreams of infinitely scalable revenue can quickly become a horrible quagmire if a managed services channel program is not properly thought out and executed.

Another byproduct from a managed services channel program is the potential for confusion and distrust on the part of the channel partners when they see that a fellow colleague has now become a vendor. The camaraderie and shared experiences that bind fellow service providers together can vanish in an instant when they perceive that one of their own is now trying to sell to them. Many MSPs believed that their intimacy and proximity to a potential group of resellers will be enough to ensure success. What these MSPs typically fail to consider is how that relationship will change almost in an instant when the reseller community realizes that instead of a colleague they now have a company that wants to sell them something. More importantly, resellers tend to talk amongst themselves and can spread the word about an MSP's new business model very quickly throughout the channel.

What you should take away from all this is that a poorly planned managed services channel strategy can quickly become a disaster. Not only will your hopes for a powerful channel crumble but so will your end-user customer base as well.

While there are countless examples of MSPs partnering with one another there are very few examples of MSPs who have successfully developed a channel program that produced any significant amount of revenue. One other thought to consider is the inevitable lifecycle of a reseller. The reason many MSPs have been enamored with the idea of developing a managed services channel is because of the sheer number of new entrants into the managed services industry. However, as these new entrants become educated and ultimately self-sufficient they will quickly realize that they can make more money by delivering the managed services themselves as opposed to selling someone else's.

In the end, offering your managed services to resellers is inherently unstable.[14] Any MSP thinking that they will create a 100% channel driven managed services business should really consider the long-term plans of their channel partners and whether or not they want to invest in a group that will ultimately grow out of the relationship.

There are plenty of theories when it comes to reselling managed services. Many of these theories are put forth by companies who seek to offer their own managed services to the channel. Whatever your views on reselling managed services this chapter should provide you with enough information to

---

14 This refers only to those MSPs whose entire revenue source comes from a reseller model.

implement a viable and sound channel program that does not put your entire managed services revenue at risk.

DON'T NOC IT
UNTIL YOU'VE TRIED IT

The question of whether or not to build a network operation center (NOC) has been at the heart of the managed services debate for several years now. The first generation of MSPs came from an era where building a NOC was essential to offering managed services. NOCs were almost always funded by venture capital due to the often large expense of building them. Although the NOCs differed in size, dimensions, grandeur, and technical wizardry, the overall objective of building a NOC was to have a central facility from which to monitor and manage a client's IT. It is not the purpose of this chapter to provide an architectural template for how to build a NOC. Rather, the purpose of this chapter is to reinforce the benefits of having a NOC and to provide a structured operational model for those MSPs who choose not to build a NOC.

While today it is still commonly held that having a NOC is the best way to deliver managed services there are new and exciting methods that are not so much challenging the old ways but reinventing them. Today, many smaller companies entering the managed services profession lack the financial resources their older colleagues possessed. Naturally, high cost items like a NOC tend to become sacrificed for other items of greater perceived value to the MSP. Adding to the debate are larger MSPs who have the funds to build a NOC (or have already built a NOC) who integrate a virtual NOC model into their managed services practice. Because the mainstream IT standards have never addressed the issue of facilities versus non-facilities based managed services it has fallen on managed services professional associations, like the MSPAlliance, to create standards that reconcile these two seemingly opposed operational models.[15]

WHAT MAKES A NOC?

No matter on which side of the issue you stand there are few who would dispute that a facilities based managed services operational model offers the most security and control for the client. The rationale behind building a NOC should be evident. The NOC, if built and operated correctly, provides an enclosed and impenetrable space for the MSP to view its managed services operations. Think of it as a mission control center where the MSP not only views the client's IT network but also manages all the activity taking place across the MSP's entire network of clientele. For many years the NOC has come to represent one of the central characteristics of MSPs.

Naturally, in order to be effective the NOC must possess certain characteristics. These characteristics, while each MSP has their own interpretation, tend to be quite similar when compared side by side. Again, this section is not meant to be

---

15 A conscious attempt was made not to make this book an overt sales pitch for any particular IT standard. However, in this chapter, reference to the Managed Services Accreditation Program was unavoidable as it is the only managed services specific model that addresses the use of network operation centers and viable alternatives to their non-use.

the definitive guide to building a NOC. Instead, this section should illustrate the important business and technological objectives served by having a well constructed and operated NOC.

Security

A NOC must be secure. But what does this mean? Many smaller MSPs have visions of very large and expensive NOCs and as a result of these preconceived notions never undertake building a NOC of their own. In actuality, a NOC does not have to cost millions of dollars in order to be effective. A NOC should be enclosed; it should be limited only to those employees who have access to client networks. Furthermore, the facility should have security controls in place to ensure that only those authorized employees are actually entering the NOC. This means you must have locks that work and people watching those technicians who enter and leave the facility.

Backups and Redundancy

A NOC built on sand is worthless. The NOC has come to represent stability, security, and integrity for those MSPs possessing one as well as to those clients who rely on them. A well built NOC should take into account the natural order of things, including how unforeseen problems can occur throwing an MSP's entire world into chaos. Natural occurrences like earthquakes, storms, and even power disruption, can wreak havoc on an unsuspecting MSP. Redundant Internet connectivity and backup power are just a few of the characteristics that will make a NOC truly viable and effective.

Sharing of the Minds

A NOC can do more than just provide physical security and other backup and redundant capabilities. A properly run NOC can offer an MSP something far more important than technological benefits; I am talking about the collaboration of an MSP's technicians in a central location working together to solve problems. Technicians who are physically proximate to one another can not only work together in solving client issues but they can also share information that furthers the collective education of the MSP. As an MSP, one of the most important traits the company can possess is education and expertise related to technology and business. Sharing information via email and through other methods is no match for being in the same room.

BUILDING A VIRTUAL NOC

As we have discussed, many new MSPs (primarily those servicing the SMB market) are choosing to forego building a physical NOC in favor of constructing a virtual NOC. You may be wondering what is involved in building a virtual NOC for it is a very natural and good question to ask. In order to answer this important question it is necessary to consult the Managed Services Accreditation Program (MSAP) as this is the only existing template addressing how MSPs should employ a virtual NOC in a managed services environment.

The MSAP outlines the use of a virtual NOC as well as basic security and operational guidelines for technicians as they travel. The challenge of operating an MSP with a virtual NOC is that of maintaining adequate security. As virtual NOC technicians openly enter and leave the office, often traveling to client sites, going home, and other locations, keeping accurate security logs, physical security (on the laptops and other handheld devices they use), and maintaining high standards of managed services excellence can be difficult. For this reason, the MSP must implement certain protocols that ensure the integrity of client data. Use of encryption technologies, strong authentication, poison pill technology, and other forms of common sense should be easily affordable by even the smallest of MSPs.

What this means in practicality is that a technician taking a laptop used for monitoring a client should be guarded jealously, both in the MSP's office and outside it. The MSP must have a mechanism for auditing the work performed by its technicians wherever they may be. In short, many of the same security and audit procedures employed in running a physical NOC should also be used in operating a virtual NOC. What are missing are the physical security and redundancy backups that only a physical NOC can provide. Having a virtual NOC, while it may be growing in popularity, does offer more opportunities for a breakdown in the managed services service delivery process.

Obviously, whether or not the MSP using a virtual NOC model offers 24x7 monitoring will be dependent on the number of hours they are available to their clients. There are very few who believe that simply being on duty (as defined by being accessible by phone and email) is not enough to constitute being a 24x7 MSP. And while there are examples of MSPs operating true 24x7 virtual NOCs, it is important that smaller MSPs not yield to temptation by claiming to possess this capacity when they do not.

BUILD VS. PARTNER

This brings us to an important part of the book that is consuming the attention of many young entrants to the managed services profession. Even with the opportunity to build a robust virtual NOC there are some MSPs who are deciding to partner with an existing MSP in order to leverage that MSP's NOC. The discussion of benefits and disadvantages of partnering with another MSP has already been covered in a different section of this book. Yet, the decision to partner with another MSP strictly in order to access a physical NOC is important enough to warrant its own section.

Typically, young MSPs enter into these partnerships primarily for reasons having nothing to do with the existence of a physical NOC. But whatever the reason, MSPs should weigh heavily this decision as it can have dangerous repercussions. In the end, it is difficult to advise everyone about which path is the right one as each company's situation is unique. However, if a company decides to partner with an MSP with a NOC then choosing a partner that has passed the Managed Services Accreditation Exam is one of the best methods of selecting a qualified and secure MSP. In these situations, selecting the wrong MSP can have very negative and far reaching implications. This is especially true where there are many companies holding themselves out as experienced MSPs when in fact they are not. Particularly in an era when greater transparency and disclosure are becoming the norm, choosing a non-accredited MSP can greatly impact, in a negative manner, a young MSP's managed services career.

No matter what your decision, whether you build your own physical NOC, whether you construct a virtual NOC, or whether you partner with another MSP, the network operation center will continue to be the engine that runs a managed services practice.

MERGERS, ACQUISITIONS, AND OTHER CONCEPTS

In a former life I used to have an M&A firm that specialized in MSPs. It was a difficult profession and one that did not suit my personal tastes. I did, however, learn quite a lot about the managed services industry and about mergers and acquisitions. One of the things I learned was that it is very difficult to create a successful transaction between two companies. Both parties need to see eye to eye on the big issues, frequently compromising on many smaller issues. Over the years, there have been relatively few M&A deals involving MSPs that made much sense (in my opinion). Many such deals were formed out of desperation or ignorance. The purpose of this chapter is to provide a perspective on the effectiveness of M&A in the managed services industry, both for buyers and sellers. Knowing that all executives have some exit strategy for their company, M&A often becomes an option. Having the right information about what M&A can or cannot do will provide you will help advise you as you consider your own company's exit strategy.

VALUATIONS

As we previously discussed the issue of company valuations tends to be a very tricky topic during an M&A transaction. Sellers naturally think that their company is worth more than it really is while buyers usually discount the worth of the target below its actual value. Somewhere in the middle the two parties must meet in order to conclude the deal. With the increasing number of companies choosing to resell managed services I believe it is important to discuss this topic as it relates to an M&A strategy.

Companies who choose to resell managed services may have their reasons for embarking down this path. However, if the company has no long term strategy for bringing those managed services in house then a financial readjustment must take place. What I mean by this is that if a reseller hopes to realize a significant price for their company simply because they are reselling another MSP's managed services they will be frequently upset. Unless a company has the contract that says they own the client there is very little increased corporate valuation that will remain with them. I have personally witnessed buyers look at an MSP's financial books and discount, item by item, all the revenue that was not tied to a contrFair or not, this is a very common and wise practice in the managed services world. If the acquiring company cannot buy the contract then that client has very little value. The chance of the client switching MSPs after the deal become very real if there is no contract to hold them to it.

In order to maximize your company's valuation make sure that any managed services revenues have a corresponding contract. This practice will ensure that you get the most out of your company when you decide to sell.

M&A LIABILITY

Putting together the right M&A transaction can be very rewarding if done properly. Done incorrectly, the parties can find themselves worse off than they were before the deal. One of the ways this can happen is when the acquiring company fails to conduct its due diligence on the acquisition candidate. Naturally, financial due diligence must take place. Checking the books, having accountants review everything, these are natural steps to any M&A transaction. What I am referring to is the failure of the buyer to adequately investigate the selling company's internal practices, its security methods, and anything that might compromise the relationship after it has been consummated.

In an industry as sensitive as managed services it is important for the buyer of an MSP firm to perform a thorough investigation so that they are not buying needless and unwanted headaches down the road. This may seem like a simple concept but in a majority of deals, especially smaller deals, very few companies do this task very well. If you are buying an MSP you might want to know if they are abiding by all the appropriate security practices. Naturally, as a buyer you would want to know if the MSP you wanted to buy was delivering a majority of its services via a reseller model. Knowledge of this sort might materially affect your opinion of the company and its worth.

Performing the appropriate amount of investigation into the company with whom you plan to do business is simply a smart business practice. Buying a company that has skeletons in its closet can mean even bigger problems later on when they are discovered. Through adequate preparation these situations can often be avoided.

M&A TRENDS IN THE MANAGED SERVICES INDUSTRY

Predicting the future is difficult and I do pretend to be able to do it. However, having been in this industry for a fair amount of time I believe that there are certain trends that can be analyzed, thereby allowing us to make fairly accurate guesses at what is likely to come in the next few years. The first few years of this century saw an increase in M&A activity that was primarily fueled by starvation and desperation. Starvation came from the rapidly shrinking revenues while the desperation came from the frantic belief that only a cash rich buyer would be able to salvage a failing business. This activity produced many erroneous predictions about the managed services industry at the time. Primarily, there were a lot of analysts and consultants making predictions that over the next few years there would only be a few remaining MSPs left. I feel it is safe to say that this prediction was incorrect.

Today, with so many new entrants to the managed services profession there are some who are predicting that there will be another wave of consolidation very soon. I agree. However, I do not think this consolidation will occur for at least another couple of years. The amount of interest in managed services today, both in the channel and amongst consumers, is on the rise. While this rise continues only the extremely desperate or those who simply want to cash out of the managed services profession will attempt to sell. In a few years, when the smaller MSPs have tried their hand at this profession there will likely be a large wave of smaller deals taking place as mostly larger MSPs attempt to gain clients via acquisition. While I do not believe that such a motive is a good reason to buy a company, there are those that will feel this way and act on their beliefs.

It is also safe to assume that MSP valuations will increase as well. As long as the revenues are tied to a contract, the profit margins are where they should be, and due diligence has been performed, sellers should see a healthy increase in their valuation multiples. Over the next several years, for the astute observer there will be many opportunities to buy some good companies in the managed services industry. While it is very difficult to identify these deals, it is often even more difficult to successfully complete a transaction. Having the right expectations when entering an M&A deal is useful. More often than not a merger or acquisition will fall apart before the final paperwork is signed. Although the right M&A deal can do a lot of good for a company there is no substitute for growing your managed services practice organically.

HARDWARE AS A SERVICE

The term Hardware as a Service (HaaS) is one that has come into common usage during the last one to two years. While it is picking up momentum as a viable and legitimate model it is not a new concept to the managed services industry. Simply put, Hardware as a Service is nothing more than leasing under a fancy new name.

For many years VARs have been using a variety of leasing models in order to increase their product sales. Immediately after the dotcom crash hardware sales began to suffer and IT providers began to seriously consider the move towards managed services. Now, after several strong years of IT spending increases and widespread adoption of managed services MSPs are employing HaaS as a mechanism for bundling both hardware and managed services under one recurring bill.

But HaaS is much more than just a ploy to add more hardware revenue to a company's bottom line, it is a mechanism that can actually produce beneficial results to an MSP's managed service practice. HaaS allows an MSP to deliver both services and hardware to a client under one monthly bill. Clients typically like this arrangement because they have a simplified

IT bill. But simplified billing and new equipment are but a few of the benefits to be realized from HaaS. Standardization is the real benefit from a HaaS approach to managed services.

MSPs have long been plagued by client networks that are difficult to maintain. Many of these problems tend to be caused by client interference. As many MSPs can attest, meddling clients can consume a lot of time and resources. Some of these problems can be solved by education while others require a more stringent approach. Clients often have networks that are comprised of hardware and software of varying sorts. Different operating systems and applications, running on different model PCs, networked by different types of servers and networking gear, are very common in many small and medium sized business environments. These disparate networks cause a lot of problems for MSPs, especially when coupled with clients who do not want to consider a massive network upgrade.

HaaS is providing an answer to this problem. One of the common reasons clients voice to large network upgrades is cost. Inability to reconcile the benefits of a homogeneous network with the large capital expenditure is a very real problem for MSPs who are trying to help their clients bring their IT spending and performance under control. As is often the case in SMB IT environments, clients using a reacting IT management process will have IT costs that are greater than those found under a managed services model. Because the IT expenditures are spread out SMB executives tend to believe that their IT costs are under control. However, what these executives fail to realize or account for is the drastic underperformance of their IT and the employees who rely on that technology.

Even those SMB executives who do not feel the financial pinch of reactive IT management eventually realize the effects on employee performance. The task of many MSPs is getting their clients to understand how a regimented managed IT service can radically improve their businesses. In these situations MSPs will commonly recommend installing a standardized IT environment. Such a network would have similar hardware gear not to mention similar operating systems and applications. These standardized networks allow MSPs to more effectively manage the IT experience for their clients by eliminating problems and improving time to resolution. Having clients that have similar equipment translates into a much easier time managing their IT.

A HaaS model whereby the MSP sells a client on similar hardware and software and plans for periodic hardware refreshes actually has a better chance of a higher gross profit margin. Products that are constantly being refreshed under the management of the MSP will have less likelihood of breaking and the MSP will have a much easier time resolving problems when they do occur. Clients experience a greater level of performance from their IT and never have to rely on old or outdated hardware ever again. Better still, these clients are able to have predictable IT expenditures along with their predictable IT performance. Everybody wins.

There are still many in the MSP industry who believe that HaaS is simply a mechanism for delivering more products but hopefully this chapter has demonstrated that the benefits from a HaaS model are far more widespread and meaningful, to both the client and the MSP.

ETHICS IN THE MANAGED SERVICES PROFESSION

When you talk about ethics in the technology industry many people tend to view it as oil and water; two things that really have nothing to do with one another. I would suggest that ethics and the managed services industry have everything to do with one another. In fact, it is the ethical obligations held by many professional MSPs that distinguish them from the IT service providers. This chapter is meant to give the reader both a sense of the ethical obligations MSPs must adhere to as well as deal with some of the more advanced ethical theories that are slowly making their way into the managed services profession.

Because there is no existing legal codification of an MSP's obligations to its clients many of the issues dealt with in this chapter are, in fact, theoretical. It is the belief of many in the industry that MSPs will eventually become regulated similar to the legal, accounting and medical professions. While we can only wait until that day happens, the sooner MSPs become self regulated and accustomed to the obligations (both legal and ethical) they have to their clients the better off they will be.

WHY ETHICS?

When I speak to companies, both MSPs and companies looking to become MSPs, there are some who are just plain confused as to why I would mention ethics. I suppose it is possible that some of these individuals think it is rudimentary or simplistic to talk about behaving well when conducting business. Obviously, this is something that we all must do no matter what our line of business is. What I mean when I say MSPs must have ethics when dealing with their clients I mean that they have obligations that go well beyond simple rules of decorum and etiquette.

Because of their unique relationship with clients MSPs have access to very sensitive components of their client's IT infrastructure. This access demands that the MSP behave in a way that goes well beyond what is expected of any business. The MSP who takes on the responsibility for managing the IT infrastructure for their clients must be held to a standard that is higher than normal businesses.

For example, if we walk into an auto parts store we would all expect that everyone from the owner all way down to the lowest employee would conduct themselves in a professional manner. Because we live in a civilized society we have these expectations even when dealing with nonprofessional businesses. When we enter a doctor's office we have the same expectations. We expect that everyone we encounter will at least attempt to behave in a friendly and professional manner. However, when we enter that doctor's office we also have the expectation that we will receive professional services that exceed basic etiquette and good business practices. As patients, we expect that we will receive impartial advice, advice that is designed to make us healthier, and advice that is not tainted or in any way influenced by any other outside party. It goes without saying that we as patients expect that our conversations with our physicians will also be kept confidential. These are things we do not even have to ask of our physicians because we have already been educated that this is how doctors should behave. We know that doctors have taken the Hippocratic Oath that dictates how they should treat their patients. Many other professions (like legal, accounting, engineering, and others) have similar ethical and professional obligations that dictate how they should act.

These distinctions make a difference to consumers. We, as consumers, like to know that our needs our being met by experts; people who not only have knowledge above the rest of us but will dispatch that knowledge in a way that is governed by rules that ensure the integrity of that industry. All of these things make us feel good about doing business with these professionals. This is what sets the managed services industry apart from the rest of the reactive IT management industry. MSPs not only have education and expertise when it comes to IT management but they are also held to a much higher standard. MSPs are expected to not only know how to manage IT but they are also expected to provide their clients with professional counsel that exceeds the level of service provided other types of IT providers.

The managed services profession has achieved a level of credibility and distinction in the technology industry that is beyond dispute. No longer are MSPs looked at as fringe players in the IT management realm. Part of the reason for this coming-of-age has to do with the ethical obligations and standards that the managed services industry has placed on itself; obligations that had nothing to do with prompting by outside bodies. Wherever you may be in your managed services career it may be worth it to evaluate your own company and the ethical and professional obligations you owe to your clients. Not only will exhibiting such behavior distinguish you from the rest of the reactive IT world but will also ensure the longevity and success of the managed services industry for many years to come.

ETHICAL RULES AND GUIDELINES FOR MSPS

As previously stated, there are no legal guidelines specific to the managed services profession.[16] While it is likely a matter of time before some governmental body decides to regulate the MSP community the industry has really been left up to its own to police itself and ensure the protection and well-being of the managed services client. In an attempt to provide the foundations for self governance industry groups like the MSPAlliance have created rules and guidelines that can be used by MSPs and their clients to ensure the integrity of this trusted relationship. Because the technology industry changes so quickly it is very

---

16 Other than those regulating managed services clients.

difficult to predict which issues will be of interest even a few months into the future. Regardless of how quickly technology changes there are some basic ethical and professional guidelines that every MSP, regardless of their nationality, size, or make up, should be able to follow.

Impartiality

Providing your clients with impartial advice is important for MSPs. Being free of any conflict of interest allows the MSP to deliver its services without the risk of influence tainting the relationship. Clients expect to get neutral advice from their MSPs. What this means is the MSP needs to begin operating its business with a little more autonomy from vendors than they have in years past. MSPs can no longer allow outside relationships (with vendors or partners) to unfairly influence the advice and counsel they provide to their clients. Being knowledgeable about one or two vendors and their technology can be a good thing. This knowledge can really help a client. However, when the relationship with that vendor becomes overbearing to the point it harms the client, it is up to the MSP to do the right thing. The true power of an MSP lies in its ability to make unbiased recommendations to its clients.

Confidentiality

Because of the unique access MSPs have with their client's IT networks it is only natural to expect that certain sensitive information will become known to the MSP during the course of the relationship. What is done with this information is what sets the MSP apart from the rest of the IT service provider world.

There are many situations in which the MSP will become aware of the most intimate activities of their clients. MSPs need to be able to keep certain information private between the client and the MSP. This privilege will enable MSPs to perform their duties without having to compromise their clients. Clients, on the other hand, will be more likely to entrust their MSP with information if they know the MSP will not be discussing such things with third parties.

The following are some basic examples of how an MSP could stumble across sensitive client information. During law school and medical school professors employ these hypothetical scenarios help their students create a moral, ethical, and psychological framework that will serve them throughout their careers. Contemplating what you would do in these situations will help you immensely as you service your clients.

IT audits are frequently performed by MSPs, both at the beginning of the relationship and periodically throughout the life of the managed services contract. The reasons for conducting these audits can be numerous. At the beginning of the relationship the MSP has a legitimate need to assess the state of the client's network. Simply asking the client will almost never yield accurate results so the MSP needs to conduct their own due diligence and come to their own conclusions about the IT network they are being asked to manage. These audits, while of obvious use to both parties at the beginning of the relationship, are also very useful later on so the MSP can ensure that nothing has crept into the network that might compromise it.

When the MSP conducts such an audit they often obtain large amounts of information about the client's business, including information that may be embarrassing or sensitive to the client. For example, during the course of a routine IT audit the MSP could easily discover that the client does not have enough licenses for the software they have installed. In this situation, the MSP should probably disclose to the client that they are at risk of being sued by the Business Software Alliance and that they should probably come up with a strategy to not only resolve the licensing conflict but also to prevent such things from happening in the future.

During the course of managing a client's network an MSP can become quite familiar with the client's business, including the employees, their customers, and many other aspects of the client's operations. There are several known cases where an MSP has uncovered wrongdoing on the part of their client's employees. In these situations, there are several paths available to the MSP, each with their own outcomes. The decision you would make in any of these situations is something that should be discussed amongst your employees so they understand their obligations should something like this occur.

The first likely scenario involves accidental behavior. What this usually means is someone in the client company does something that could compromise the company. Typically, these situations involve loss of corporate intellectual property.

Company databases, formulas, trade secrets, anything of value to the company that is in electronic form could potentially become compromised. What makes these events more unfortunate is that they can happen by pure accident, absence any malice or intention on the part of the employee. Databases can be left open, corporate firewalls penetrated, wireless access points exposed, along with countless other security holes that could be used to leak out important information. The situations where an employee accidentally exposes corporate information are even more damaging because the chances of anyone learning about the exposure can be very low.[17]

While most of the data breaches that occur happen from within the company not all of these are innocent or by accident. Disgruntled employees tend to make the most likely suspects in these situations but whatever their motivations the damage they can do to their employers and the general public is considerable. Employers who do not have adequate safety measures in place to prevent or at the very least know about internal data breaches run the risk of legal liability and loss of trust by the public.

MSPs are in a unique position to be able to identify and prevent such data breaches from happening by implementing the appropriate security controls. Naturally, the MSP should disclose such a breach to the client. But, what additional obligations does the MSP have with regards to disclosing the activities they uncover? For example, in this scenario would the MSP have an obligation to notify the authorities about the data

---

17 Uncovering corporate data breaches, either intentional or unintentional, rarely occur unless the company has an effective IT management mechanism in place.

breach? In at least half of the United States there are data breach notification laws that mandate disclosure of such breaches to the relevant authorities. Making disclosures because it is the law is one thing, but should the MSP keep such a data breach in confidence with regards to others?

What if an MSP identifies employee misconduct (such as sexual harassment) not involving a data breach? In this situation, there would be no law or obligation to disclose the incident to authorities. However, the MSP would have an obligation to the client to let them know what they found. It would be conceivable that the client would want to know of such employee misconduct. But, having the MSP talk about what they found with outside individuals would be a devastating blow to the client. The client would naturally expect that the MSP would be discrete and not tell anyone (except if compelled by the authorities).

The influence of the MSP in today's corporate culture is powerful indeed. As MSPs and managed services become more commonplace in the global business community the obligations that MSPs have to their clients should become more defined. Until then, MSPs would be well served to construct their own rules of confidentiality and make those rules known to their clients.

Expertise

One of the reasons other professions like legal and medical have very little problems marketing themselves is that, as an industry, they have educated the general public in such a way that people know instinctively who they should call when they have a particular problem. For instance, most people understand that when they are sick they should go to a doctor. Likewise, when people have legal problems they instinctively know to seek out the advice and counsel of an attorney. The same can be said of other professions like engineers, architects, accountants, etc. All of these professional industries have worked hard over the years to educate the public and the fruits of their labor have paid high dividends. When attorneys and doctors begin their practices they do so knowing that all they need to do is let the general public know who and where they are. Once that has been accomplished the rest will take care of itself.

The reason this combination of education and marketing works is because of the expertise inherent in all of these professions. Everybody knows that doctors, attorneys, and accountants all have special training and expertise when it comes to the performance of their professional duties. We all know that going to a plumber when we have legal problems simply does not make sense because the plumber, while an expert at plumbing, is not an expert when it comes to legal issues. The same is true with IT. MSPs have unique training and expertise when it comes to the management of IT. As an industry, MSPs only have to educate the mass public about their expertise in order to fully realize the benefits of being in a profession like managed services.

Being an expert in a particular field also allows that professional to remain focused on their core areas of expertise by making referrals to other professionals. One problem that has dogged the managed services industry for the last several years is the unwillingness of MSPs to refer clients to other MSPs. While there are mechanisms for referring clients without losing control of the client relationship MSPs need to learn how to say no to a client. Part of this issue would be resolved very quickly with the appropriate legislative intervention. For example, the issue of negligence or malpractice is a very real threat preventing doctors and lawyers from holding themselves out to be experts in a particular area of practice. Basically, both of these professions (and others) have clearly definable boundaries when it comes to taking on clients or patients. A general practitioner would never consider doing complex surgery without taking on significant legal and moral liability. For this reason, medical general practitioners will refer their patients to specialists who are experts in a particular field. Likewise, attorneys who are inexperienced in a particular field of law will make a referral to someone who is experienced in that area. At the very least, a doctor or lawyer will seek out the advice of an expert even if they do not make an actual referral.

MSPs need to learn how to incorporate outside firms when faced with situations that are beyond their own expertise. While there are no specific laws governing MSPs it is quite likely that general rules of negligence will apply to MSPs in the near future. When this occurs MSPs that hold themselves out to be experts in areas where they are not will likely get into trouble. For this reason, it is important that the managed services industry begin to self regulate itself sooner rather than later.

Disclosure

Transparency is one of the greatest traits a profession can have. There are very real disclosures that must be made by professionals if they want to do certain things. For example, lawyers wishing to serve as counsel for a particular client should disclose any conflicts of interest that may be damaging or in any way compromise that attorney's ability to fairly and vigorously represent the client. In the previous section we examined how holding oneself out to be an expert in a particular area comes with a price. Anything that might be damaging to a client should be disclosed. The same is true for the managed services profession.

Today, although it is a practice that is highly discouraged and is currently being addressed, many MSPs tend to be very protective of their clients. Being protective of a client is not necessarily a bad thing but it is if the MSP begins to hide or misrepresent their capabilities to the client for fear that they will lose faith in their abilities. This behavior tends to take place among the smaller MSPs who are building their managed services practice but it has been known to happen throughout small and large MSPs alike. Naturally, during any business start up we all tend to fight a little bit harder for clients. However, this can go too far if we begin to misrepresent our capabilities.

For example, MSPs who wish to appear capable and knowledgeable might make an assertion about having a network operations center when in fact they do not. Similarly, they might make a statement about having a datacenter that the client can use when in fact they do not have a datacenter. What is most widespread, however, are statements related to the number of hours an MSP will be available to the client while they are protecting their network. Assertions that an MSP is a 24 x 7 firm when they clearly stop working at five o'clock border on being outright falsehoods. Similarly, statements that an MSP has a particular expertise when they do not possess that expertise can also be quite damaging to the client that relies upon such statements. When it comes to the assertions they make, MSPs need to learn how to be more open and forthcoming. Because MSPs have not had a lot of government or industry oversight these activities have taken place with relatively little repercussions.

Today, however, the tide is turning and clients are becoming less and less tolerant of MSPs who make false or misleading statements. MSPs need to understand that by being more open and transparent to their clients the more likely it is the client will respect their candor and will remain trusting in the MSPs expertise and counsel. Disclosing things such as conflict of interest, methods of doing business, business partners, and other relevant pieces of information, will only help serve the long-term interests of the managed services industry.

CONCLUSION

The managed services industry has never been more vibrant than it is today and it shows no signs of stopping. While managed services have been a viable profession for the last decade there are a lot of new entrants into this profession that need guidance, support, and encouragement. At the same time, these new entrants also pose the greatest threat to the managed services profession if these young MSPs are not given the proper guidance. Ongoing cultivation of these new professionals will be critical to firming the foundation of the industry. It is essential that older MSPs meet their obligations to younger MSPs, not to give away their trade secrets, but to help foster a sense of duty and responsibility in the younger generation of MSP professionals.

The managed services industry has many challenges ahead of it. Education is chief among these as both MSPs and end-user clients must learn more about this vibrant and powerful industry. MSPs must educate themselves in order to stay relevant to the ever-changing needs of their clients. Clients need to understand how information technology can improve their businesses while at the same time appreciating the power and potential danger of their IT assets when they are unmanaged.

This is the real challenge of making IT work. End-users and MSPs must both understand where each group is coming from and attempt to meet somewhere in the middle. Clients will only continue to insert IT into their businesses. How IT is managed will determine whether technology furthers the interests of the business or gets in its way.

Another area where MSPs will have to become more proactive and diligent is the area of law and regulation. As more and more regulatory pressures are laid upon consumers all across the globe, MSPs will be called upon to alleviate these pressures. MSPs will need to become more aware of such regulatory events as well as make changes to their own internal operations in order to become capable stewards of their clients' IT assets.

The MSP community worldwide will continue to grow and prosper in years to come. There are sure to be some difficult years ahead as well. But in the end, the ever-increasing reliance on IT is sure to keep MSPs on the forefront of IT management and security. As long as this happens, the managed services profession will have a long and prosperous future.